Gem Trails of Oregon

Revised Edition

by
James R. Mitchell

Gem Guides Book Co.
315 Cloverleaf Drive, Suite F
Baldwin Park, CA 91706

Library of Congress Catalog Card Number: 98-70068
ISBN 0-935182-99-3

Maps: Jean Hammond & Richard Schoener
Cover: Paul Morrison

NOTE:
   Due to the possibility of personal error, typographical error, misinterpretation of information, and the many changes due to man or nature, *Gem Trails of Oregon, Revised Edition*, its publisher and all other persons directly or indirectly associated with this publication assume no responsibility for accidents, injury or any losses by individuals or groups using this publication.
   In rough terrain and hazardous areas all persons are advised to be aware of possible changes due to man or nature that occur along the gem trails.

TABLE OF CONTENTS

KEY TO SITES ON MAP

REGION I

Site No.

(1) Kennig
(2) Clear Creek
(3) Clackamas River
(4) The Dalles
(5) Sunflower Flat
(6) Willamette River
(7) Quartzville Creek
(8) Calapooia River
(9) Richardson's Ranch
(10) Ashwood
(11) Stein's Pillar
(12) Eagle Peak
(13) Maury Mountain
(14) Whistler Spring
(15) Biggs

REGION II

(1) Fossil
(2) White Fir Springs
(3) Wildcat Mountain
(4) Lucky Strike
(5) Highway 26
(6) Walton Lake
(7) Mitchell
(8) John Day Fossil Beds
(9) Bates
(10) Greenhorn
(11) Sumpter
(12) Baker City
(13) Emerald Creek
(14) Weiser
(15) Graveyard Point

REGION III

(1) Newberry Nat'l Volcanic Mon.
(2) Umpqua River
(3) Agness
(4) Althouse Creek
(5) Applegate North
(6) Applegate South
(7) Table Rock
(8) Gold Nugget
(9) Medford
(10) Butte Creek
(11) Agate Lake

Site No.

(12) Ashland
(13) Happy Camp
(14) Jenny Creek
(15) Lassen Creek
(16) Davis Creek
(17) Dog Lake
(18) Bear Creek

REGION IV

(1) Paulina
(2) Hampton Butte
(3) Glass Butte
(4) Riley
(5) Hines
(6) Malheur Lake
(7) Diamond Craters
(8) Buchanan
(9) White Cliffs
(10) Stinkingwater
(11) Juntura
(12) Warm Springs
(13) Drinkwater Pass
(14) Beulah Reservoir
(15) Vale
(16) Owyee
(17) Succor Creek South
(18) Succor Creek North
(19) South of Homedale
(20) Sheaville
(21) Rome
(22) McDermitt Petrified Wood
(23) McDermitt Minerals
(24) McDermitt Wonderstone
(25) Virgin Valley
(26) Big Springs
(27) Hart Mountain
(28) Plush
(29) Crane Creek
(30) Alvord Desert

REGION V

(1) Tillamook
(2) Northern Beaches
(3) Central Beaches
(4) Southern Beaches

6

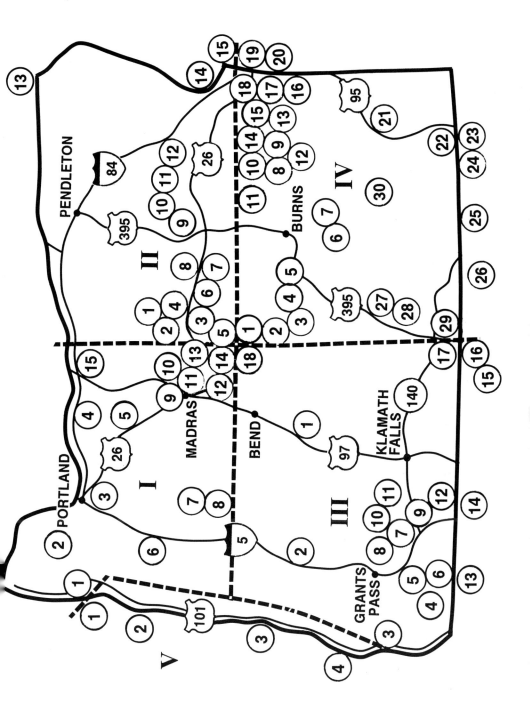

INTRODUCTION

Oregon has long been regarded as one of the country's premier rockhounding states. The sites listed on the following pages are situated in landscapes as full of variety as the minerals themselves. The terrain varies from pine covered mountains to barren desert, and should expose you to all the beauty Oregon has to offer. The completely revised *Gem Trails of Oregon* reflects many changes that have occurred since 1989 when the book was first published. A few places mentioned in the original edition have been closed and they are no longer listed. Many of the descriptions have been expanded or updated, and there are 40 completely new sites.

Each narrative includes a summary of what can be found, collecting suggestions, travel instruction, and is accompanied by a map. Mileage is as accurate as possible, but odometers on all vehicles vary and distances have been rounded to the nearest tenth of a mile. A few of the sites are general regions, sometimes encompassing a considerable area, with no particular, specific, pinpointed place of unusually high mineral or fossil concentration. Such spots can be frustrating to some, but they do provide a chance to explore interesting parts of Oregon while still having an opportunity to obtain some fine specimens.

Many of the more popular collecting localities are being depleted and the best material is disappearing rapidly. If you are patient and flexible with a willingness to put out a little extra effort, even those places can be fruitful and may be a highlight of your rockhounding trip.

A few of the sites listed on the following pages have not actually been visited by the author, but are provided as a result of very reliable information. They are clearly identified in the accompanying text, but, in such cases, the mileage may be less accurate. It is important to note that the maps are intentionally **NOT DRAWN TO SCALE**. The purpose is to provide a general location setting, and to also better show travel detail near the mineral concentrations. Also be aware that a few sites are situated on the dumps of old and abandoned mines. Do not, under any circumstances, enter the shafts and always be cautious when exploring the surrounding regions. There are often hidden tunnels, rotten ground, and pits, as well as rusty nails, broken glass and discarded chemicals, all of which create potential hazards.

Occasionally, the best collecting may be partially or totally on private property. Be sure to obtain permission to collect in these areas **BEFORE** doing so. Be willing to pay the landowner a fee if it is requested. Fee information and land status are discussed as of the time of the author's most recent visit, shortly before publication. **DO NOT ASSUME THAT THIS GUIDE GIVES PERMISSION TO COLLECT!** Land status changes frequently. If you have a suspicion that a particular site is no longer open, be sure to confirm that before trespassing. If nothing can be determined locally, land ownership information is available at the County Recorder's office.

Collectors are reminded of government regulations about collecting petrified wood. Rockhounds can obtain no more than 25 pounds of wood per day, plus one piece, and no more than 250 pounds per year. To obtain a specimen weighing more than 250 pounds, a permit must be procured from the District Manager of the Bureau of Land Management. Groups cannot pool their allocations together to obtain pieces weighing more than 250 pounds and wood from public lands cannot be bartered or sold to commercial dealers and may only be obtained with hand tools.

Most of the areas discussed in the book are easy to reach, but road conditions do change. Severe weather can make good roads very rough, and very rough roads totally impassable, even with four-wheel drive. You must decide for yourself what your particular vehicle is capable of doing.

Generally, Oregon can get quite cold and wet during the winter months. Except for the eastern lowlands and Pacific Ocean beach sites, even the spring and fall can be cool. For that reason, most of Oregon is best explored, from a rockhounding point of view, during the warmer summer months.

When venturing into some of the more remote areas, it is a good idea to take extra drinking water, foul weather clothing, and some food, just in case you get delayed or stuck. If you take the time to properly plan your trip and make sure your vehicle is in good working order, the gem fields listed on the following pages will provide you and your family with countless hours of collecting pleasure, some outstanding mineral specimens and many memorable experiences.

James R. Mitchell

The mineral of interest at this location is augite, a silicate of calcium, magnesium, iron and aluminum. The Keenig Creek material exhibits nice, but small, prismatic crystallization. It is generally black, but some has a slight greenish tone, looking very much like a dark occurrence of diopside.

Be advised that the author has not yet personally visited this spot, but the information has been provided by reliable sources. To get there, take Cedar Butte Road north from Highway 6, which intersects seven-tenths of a mile east of milepost 17. There is a sign just off the pavement designating this as the road to Keenig Creek Campground, and it is about fifty-five miles west of Portland and seventeen miles east of Tillamook. Follow Cedar Butte Road five and seven-tenths miles and then turn left onto the road to Kilchis Lookout Tower. Continue another two-tenths of a mile and some rough ruts will be seen leading down the hill on the right. It is suggested that you park at this intersection and simply hike the rest of the way. If, however, you have a rugged vehicle, you can turn onto the ruts and proceed another one-tenth of a mile.

From there, a faint trial leads up the hill on the left. Follow that switchback path about 100 yards to the base of the easily spotted butte. The primary mineralization is on the steep cliffs, making access inherently dangerous. Instead of risking injury, be content with what can be found down below. Throughout the gravel and rock at the base of the cliffs you can find plenty of the dark little augite crystals, some still intact within the native rock. You can either sort through the rubble with a shovel or hand trowel, or attempt

breaking off pieces of rock from easily accessible portions of the cliff itself. If you attack the native rock, just be careful not to dislodge something from higher up which could tumble down. This is a very scenic portion of the Tillamook State Forest. There are many good places to camp along the picturesque Wilson River, if you want to spend some time.

The Wilson River

KEENIG CREEK

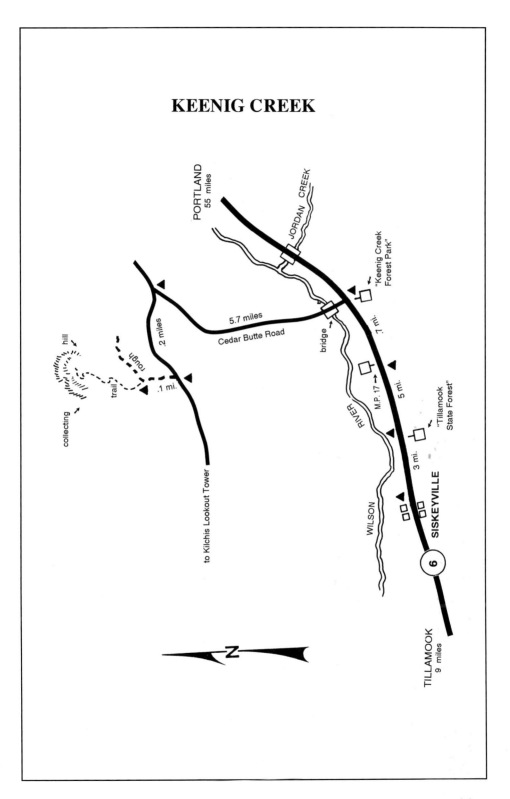

The two locations illustrated on the accompanying map offer collectors an opportunity to gather marine fossils, good quality jasper, as well as carnelian, banded, iris and plume agate. To get to there, take Highway 26 west from Portland about twenty-nine miles to Highway 47. Go north on Highway 47 five and nine-tenths miles to an old railroad bridge. Pull off into the parking lot located shortly after passing under the bridge. This is the Tophill Trailhead parking area. The collecting site, however, is on the opposite side of the highway and accessed by walking along the Banks Vernonia Linear Park Trail until reaching the railroad tracks. Just after the tracks, another lesser trial leads off to the right to an old quarry. It is within that quarry that rockhounds can find well preserved and nicely fossilized shells. Most can be found among the rubble in and around the quarry and in other exposed nearby regions. Do not dig into the quarry walls themselves, since such activity could be hazardous.

To get to the next site, continue north on Highway 47 to Timber Road, six and seven-tenths miles farther. Turn left, and proceed at least three more miles to where a small stream will occasionally be spotted paralleling the road on the left. It is amongst the gravels of that waterway, as well as Clear Creek about ten miles from the intersection of Highway 47 and Timber Road, that collectors gather plenty of colorful jasper and agate pebbles.

There are two problems associated with rockhounding in this region, though. First, there is private property running throughout the area and the rights of property owners should be respected. If you can't gain permission to visit private areas, be sure to restrict all collecting to open areas. The second problem is that the surfaces of river rock are usually very abraded and difficult to identify. When dry, most appear very dull and uninteresting. For that reason, look for faint coloration and consider splitting any stones to show fresh, unabraded surface to evaluate the stone's true potential.

Old Railroad Bridge

CLEAR CREEK

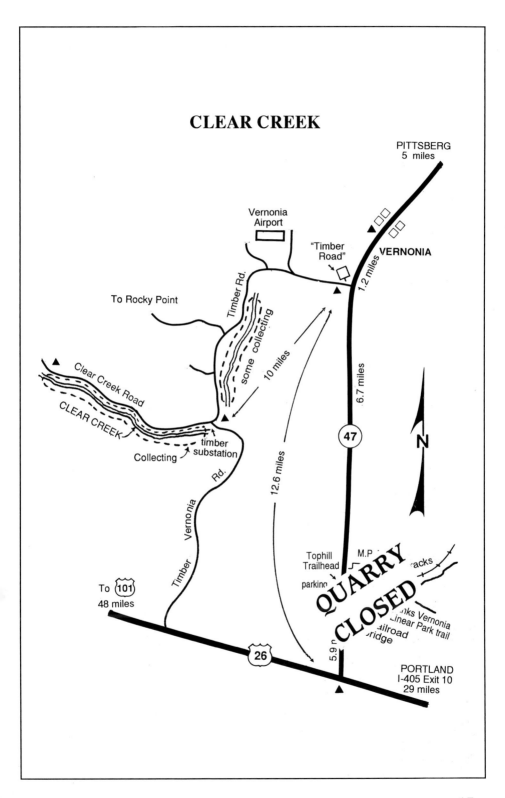

PITTSBERG
5 miles

Vernonia
Airport

"Timber
Road"

VERNONIA

To Rocky Point

Timber Rd.

some collecting

10 miles

1.2 miles

Clear Creek Road

6.7 miles

CLEAR CREEK

timber
substation

Collecting

Vernonia Rd.

12.6 miles

N

47

Timber

To 101
48 miles

Tophill
Trailhead

M.P.

racks

parking

QUARRY

CLOSED

nks Vernonia
Linear Park trail
ailroad
ridge

5.9 m

26

PORTLAND
I-405 Exit 10
29 miles

This is a general location, rather than a specific one, and features a lot of river-tumbled petrified wood, common opal, jasper and agate, as well as a very nice variety of bloodstone. In addition, one can procure fine specimens of cinnabar, generally occurring in a light colored host rock, which can be used for display in a mineral collection. To get to the west edge of this extensive site from Portland, take Exit 12 off Interstate 205 and continue east along Highway 212 for about six miles. At that point, go right onto Highway 224, approximately eighteen miles to Estacada. Just beyond town, the highway starts to parallel the Clackamas River for at least twenty more miles. It is among the gravels of the Clackamas where the wood, opal, jasper, agate and cinnabar can randomly be found. There is extensive private land between Estacada and the National Forest boundary, about seven miles farther along, making the more abundant public lands within the forest more productive places to concentrate collecting efforts.

The finest cinnabar tends to be obtained from the river and streambeds above Estacada, and rockhounding should be restricted to public lands unless permission has been granted to enter private property.

DO NOT be tempted to wade in the deep, fast flowing and sometimes dangerous river. Be satisfied with what can be found in the easily accessible gravel bars.

Just as was the case at Clear Creek, remember that river rock is usually very abraded and difficult to identify. When dry, most appear to be dull and uninteresting. For that reason, look for faint coloration and split any such stones to show a fresh, unabraded surface in order to evaluate the true potential.

CLACKAMAS RIVER

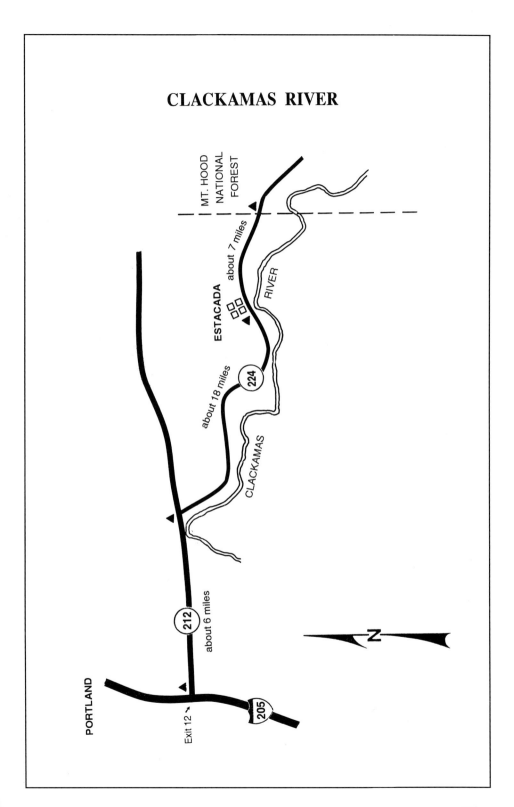

Petrified wood, agate and jasper can be found throughout regions surrounding The Dalles. Two such sites are shown on the accompanying map.

To get to Site "A," take Exit 87 off Interstate 84 and head south on Highway 197. From the Interstate and continuing a few miles along Highway 197, rockhounds can find common jasper, agate, and occasionally specimens of picture jasper. When collecting beside the highway, be sure to pull your car well off the pavement and do not enter any private lands. Material is scattered, so if nothing much is found at the first stop, simply head a little farther down the road and try again.

Site "B" is reached by passing through The Dalles and taking West 10th Street to Sevenmile Hill Road (the route to Mosier), as illustrated on the accompanying map. The best collecting seems to be the region alongside the road heading north from Sevenmile Hill Road to Ortley and Sevenmile Hill, but additional material can be found just about anywhere alongside Sevenmile Hill Road from The Dalles to Mosier. Good specimens of agate and petrified wood are haphazardly scattered for quite a distance. Pay particularly close attention to regions of erosion and allow time to do some hiking off the roads.

If you have an opportunity to explore this region shortly after a rainstorm, the distinctly colored material tends to be easier to spot. Just be sure you don't get your vehicle stuck in any mud. Take time to explore this territory for the best it has to offer. Inquire in The Dalles for information about additional local collecting spots and local road conditions.

THE DALLES

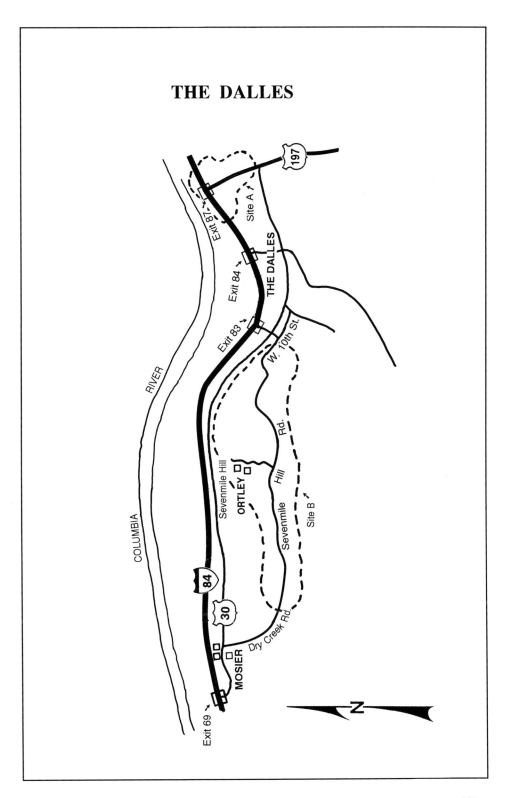

This location is on the Warm Springs Indian Reservation and AD-VANCE PERMISSION TO COLLECT MUST BE GRANTED by the Tribal Council in Warm Springs. The Tribal Council has been somewhat inconsistent over the years in regarding the issuance of collecting permits. Sometimes collecting is allowed for a fee; at other times limited permission is granted and no fee charged; yet at other times nobody is allowed to collect there. If this was not such an outstanding site, it would not be mentioned because of all the confusion; but the site's incredibly colorful agate and jasper help justify leaving a description in the book.

It is easy to tell when you are at Sunflower Flat, since there is a fenced-in area containing hundreds of sunflower plants. With or without a permit, no collecting is allowed within that fenced area, but it doesn't make much difference, since so much can be obtained from the surrounding terrain. There is green jasper, red-green jasper, green-red-orange jasper, in flows, bands and swirls, as well as clear white material with vivid banding. Small quartz crystals can also be found here, but it takes some patience and a certain degree of luck to find them.

To obtain the prized agate and jasper, simply walk through the pine covered forest paying close attention to any stone you encounter. Much of the rock here is agate and jasper. It doesn't take long to gather plenty of the beautiful cutting material from the surface, but if you want larger pieces, it is usually necessary to do some digging, if your permit allows it.

To get a quick idea what the site has to offer, walk along the road for a short distance. Smaller pieces of agate and jasper can be found lying on or beside the road. They are much easier to spot than amongst the pine needles. Roadside collecting is best done after a rainstorm or shortly after it has been graded.

If there has been recent heavy rain, it might not be advisable for vehicles without four-wheel drive to attempt visiting Sunflower Flat.

SUNFLOWER FLAT

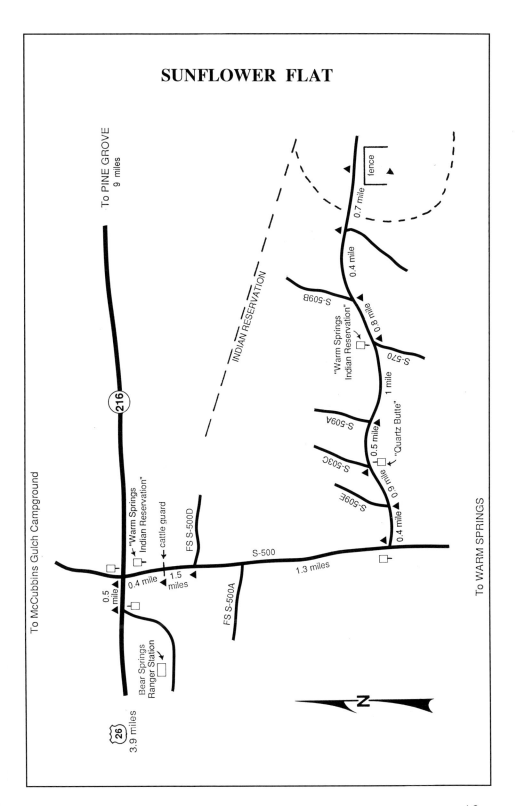

19

The gravels of the Willamette River have long provided collectors with fine specimens of colorful agate and jasper, especially in the region stretching from Salem south to Corvallis. Collecting along the Willamette is best during the summer months when the water is low, thereby often forming massive gravel bars. Some of the agates found here are incredibly colorful, having been washed from unknown deposits countless years ago. The Willamette is a powerful river and, for that reason, it is advisable not to do any wading. Be satisfied with what can be easily reached along the shore. In addition, be advised that there is private property along the river. You should never trespass without first gaining permission to do so. Local inquiry is helpful to determine best access to public areas along the river.

One of the frustrations with such a nonspecific spot is trying to determine exactly where to look. Since the position of gem bearing gravel bars changes with the weather, water current, river flow, and other factors, it is impossible to pinpoint specific gem producing spots along this very lengthy stretch of river. For that reason, this is a location for rockhounds with some time to spend and a willingness to make frequent stops for sampling. The area is generally scenic and pleasant, however, and the trip along State Road 51 and 99W can be relaxing.

As is the case with any river gravel collecting, don't forget that river rock is usually very abraded and difficult to identify. Most appears to be dull and uninteresting when dry. Look for faint coloration and split any such stones to show a fresh, unabraded surface in order to evaluate the true potential.

WILLAMETTE RIVER

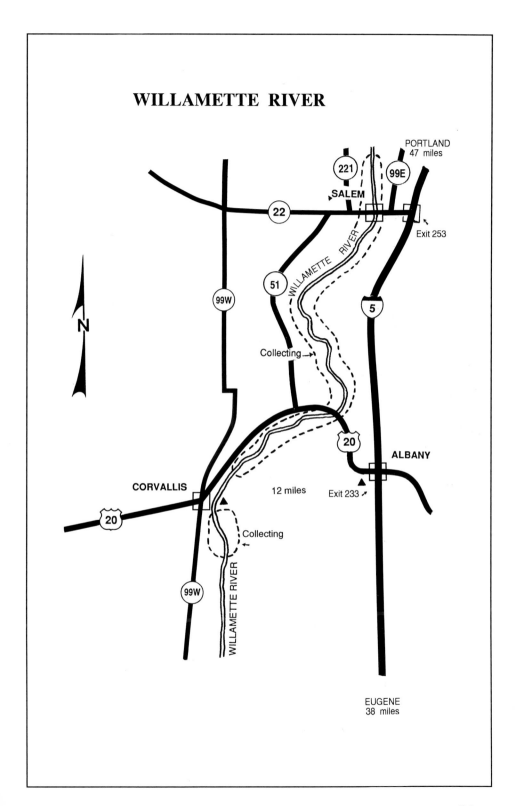

These sites are situated in one of Oregon's premier amateur gold mining areas and offer collectors the opportunity to gather some excellent mineral specimens.

Site "A" is a large basalt lava flow which contains easily spotted white, orbicular amygdules which often contain small but nice quartz, calcite and zeolite minerals. At and near Dogwood Recreation Site, labeled Site "B" on the map, one has the opportunity to pan, sluice, or dredge for gold. All along this stretch of river there is a good chance for finding color and it has become a popular place for amateur gold seekers.

Site "C" is easily spotted from the road, being a quarry on the side of the hill, only a short distance away. In that quarry, rockhounds can find pyrite, often associated with showy, radiating tourmaline crystals and occasional traces of native silver. Be very careful, if you choose to remove rock from the quarry walls, some of the upper material is rotten and easily dislodged, creating a potential hazard to those working below. You should only work in safe locations. As is the case with any mine, the ownership status can change from time to time. Always be sure to inquire locally as to the status of collecting.

Just beyond the quarry, immediately before reaching Yellowstone Creek Road, more pyrite cubes can be obtained from the iron stained, highly altered rocks on the left. In addition to pyrite, one can find small amounts of chalcopyrite and tourmaline. All three minerals occurring together often make very nice display pieces.

Follow the directions given on the accompanying map to Site "D." Continue along Boulder Creek Road as it parallels the river for about one and six-tenths miles to a road cut. In and around that road cut collectors can obtain pyrite crystals, some of which measure up to one-half inch across. Many occur as pyritohedrons, or twelve faced crystals, each of which has five sides. Native rock containing such specimens make great showpieces in a mineral collection.

Good gold panning, sluicing and dredging can be accomplished just about anywhere along Quartzville Creek or Yellowstone Creek throughout the region labeled Site "E" on the map. If you have time, continue to the site of Quartzville. Good mineral specimens can be found within the dumps on the surrounding hillsides, as well as throughout areas of erosion down below. Just be certain to stay off private claims.

Panning is unrestricted on public lands throughout the Quartzville Creek area, but you will need a permit to operate a dredge. For more information, contact the Bureau of Land Management, Salem District, 1717 Fabry Road SE, Salem, Oregon 97306; (503) 375-5646.

QUARTZVILLE CREEK

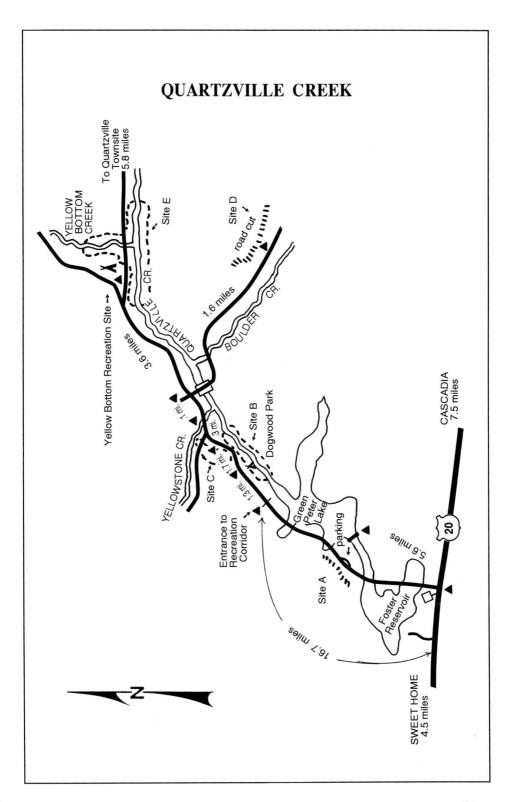

Not long ago, fine specimens of petrified wood and brilliant orange carnelian could be found in regions near Sweet Home. Rockhounds could procure vivid blue agate in the hills near Holley. Recently, however, all those deposits have been closed.

Occasional pieces of the Sweet Home and Holley material can still be found along the banks and in gravel bars associated with the Calapooia River, designated as Site "A" on the map. This is a rather extensive region of interest to only the most dedicated of collectors. The area extends for many miles along the river and no particular spot tends to be better than another. From Sweet Home, head south on Highway 228 four and six-tenths miles and, just after crossing over the river, turn east. Starting about eight miles from the highway, many smaller rivers and streams empty into the Calapooia from regions near Holley and Sweat Home, carrying with them chunks of the petrified wood, carnelian and blue agate. Much of this material is then trapped on gravel bars or washed onto the banks.

Be advised that there is private land alongside the river, especially near the highway, so you must be willing to do some driving to find promising stretches of river. When you spot one, pull well off the road and see what can be found. Just remember that river rock is usually very abraded and difficult to identify, and when dry, most appear to be dull and uninteresting. Look for faint coloration and split any such stones to show a fresh, unabraded surface to evaluate its true color and quality.

In about twenty-three miles, you will be at the National Forest boundary and Forest Road 675 heading off to the right paralleling United States Creek. This is designated as Site "B" on the map. Along United States Creek, you can pan for gold which has washed down from deposits higher up. Two miles farther along Forest Service Road 2820 there are many old mines. Many are abandoned, but some are still either active or protected by a current mining claim. Carefully examine boulders and rocks in and around the dumps associated with abandoned mines for tiny cavities filled with sparkling little quartz crystals. If you can't find an abandoned prospect, inspect rock down slope on public land.

Promising gravel bar

24

CALAPOOIA RIVER

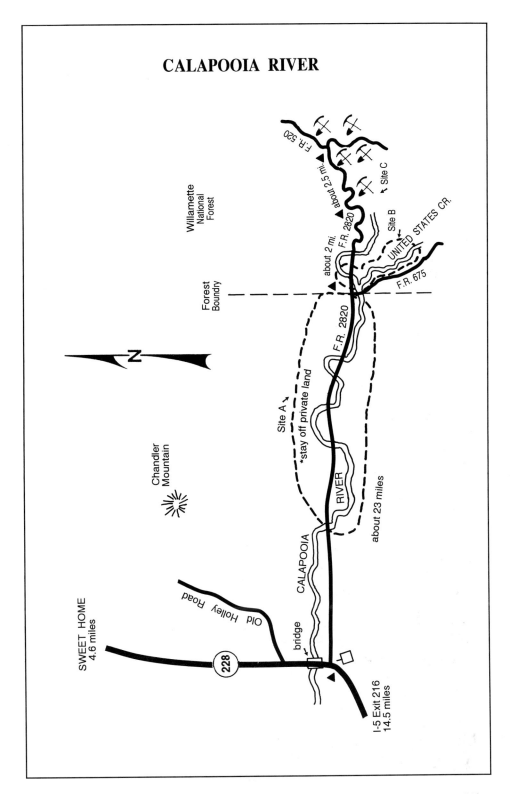

One of Oregon's best known rockhounding localities is Richardson's Recreational Ranch. Within 4,000 of the total 17,000 acre land, collectors can find thundereggs or obtain an amazing variety of agates and jaspers, and pay only for what they keep. The ranch is open all year, seven days a week, 7 a.m. to 5 p.m, weather permitting. The family owns the famous Priday and Kennedy Agate Beds. A nice meadow is provided for free overnight camping.

To get there from Madras, take Highway 97 northeast out of town to milepost 81. Just past the milepost, there is a large sign designating the turn to Richardson's Ranch. Go right, proceed two miles to yet another sign. Bear right nine-tenths of a mile more, and then left another one-tenth of a mile to the office. Here you must stop.

You can either select material at the office that has already removed from its place in the ground or you can dig it yourself. The cost is less, obviously, if you get it on your own. If you choose to dig, first register at the office. You will be given a map to the various collecting areas which include four very productive thunderegg beds, an opal bed, outcrops of moss agate, beautiful rainbow agate, flame jasper, the famous rainbow jasper ledge and the Oregon sunset jasper ledge.

Digging might sound like tough work, but the Richardsons regularly bulldoze the sites to expose fresh material, limiting the amount of actual labor necessary.

The rock shop is filled with local gemstones featuring a variety of agate, jasper and thunderegg. In addition, Richardson's produces an ingenious sphere-making machine, as well as a dry sander and polisher. Be sure to visit the shop to see some of the equipment in operation, and to view the jade carving collection and rocks from all over the world–rough and polished. The rare Chinese carvings are priceless and would be a prize for any museum. For more information, write the

Richardsons at Gateway Route, Box 440, Madras, Oregon 97741 or call (541) 475-2680 or (541) 475-2839.

Richardson's Ranch

RICHARDSON'S RANCH

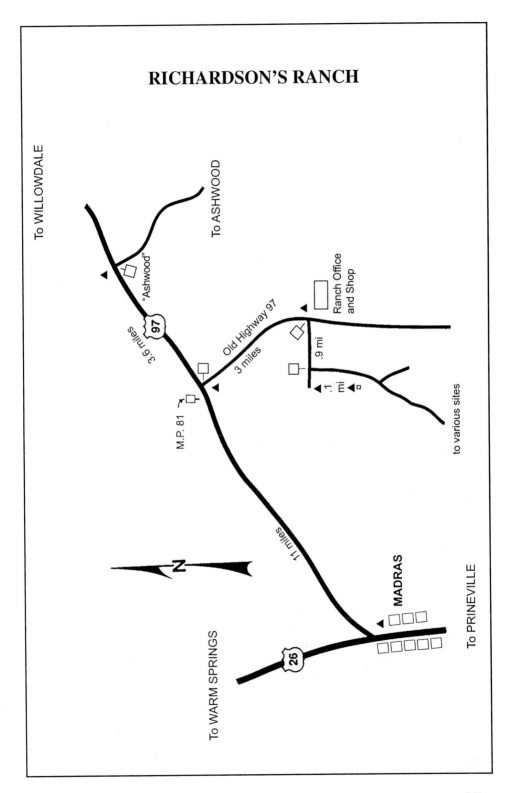

To WILLOWDALE

To ASHWOOD

"Ashwood"

97

3.6 miles

Old Highway 97

3 miles

M.P. 81

Ranch Office and Shop

.9 mi

.1 mi

to various sites

N

11 miles

To WARM SPRINGS

MADRAS

26

To PRINEVILLE

The ranches surrounding the tiny town of Ashwood are noted for their outstanding agate, jasper, petrified wood and thundereggs. This region is, without a doubt, one of the state's premier rockhounding localities. At one time, most of the local ranchers allowed collectors onto their property, but due to abuses of that privilege over the years, and the high cost of insurance, most are now closed. A few still open up to rockhounds occasionally, usually on specific dates or in conjunction with local festivals or rock and mineral shows. From year to year, however, the list of exactly which ranches will be open, and when, changes.

A few of the area ranches which have gained renown for the beautiful material that can be found within their boundaries are the Friend, Ochs (Priday), Swanson, Thorton, McDonald and Nartz Ranches. The list of what can be obtained is lengthy and includes a number of excellent thunderegg beds, as well as ledges of spectacular agate and jasper. There are digging areas where collectors can find beautiful angel wing agate, petrified wood, Keegan tube agate, Priday surprise eggs, Apache red jasper, golden pheasant jasper, Priday polka-dot agate, picture puzzle jasp-agate, rainbow ridge agate, Paulina Ridge agate and maxite.

Current information can sometimes be obtained at the Post Office in Ashwood, Oregon 97001, (541) 489-3268, or through the Chamber of Commerce in nearby Madras at 197 SE 5th Street, Madras, Oregon 97741, (541) 475-2350. Escorted rockhounding trips to the most prolific Ashwood ranches generally take place during the summer months and advance planning is mandatory.

Thundereggs from the Ashwood Area

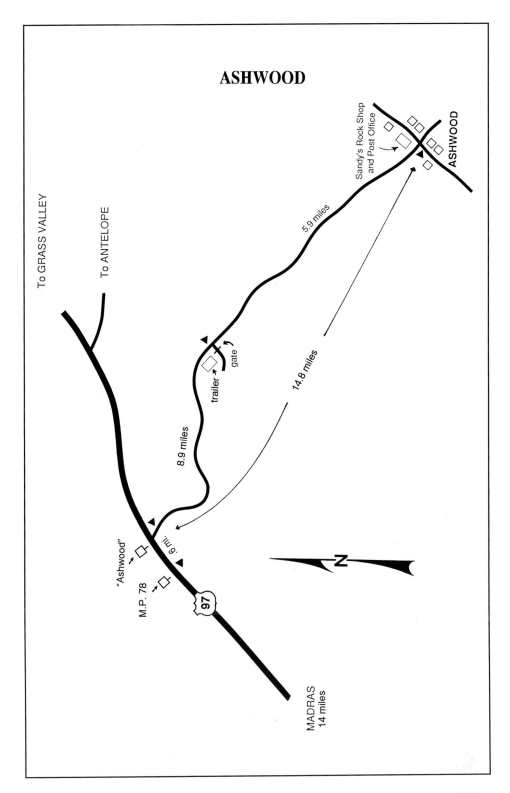

ASHWOOD

To GRASS VALLEY

To ANTELOPE

Sandy's Rock Shop
and Post Office

ASHWOOD

5.9 miles

14.8 miles

gate

trailer

8.9 miles

.6 mi.

"Ashwood"

M.P. 78

97

N

MADRAS
14 miles

This is not a collecting location, but, instead, an unusual geological formation which might be worth seeing for those with an interest in geology and mineral collecting. It also affords a fine opportunity to drive through a beautifully forested area. Stein's Pillar is a stark, light-colored rock, 120 feet in diameter, composed of three layers of welded tuff ash flows.

From Prineville, drive east on Highway 26 about nine miles to Mill Creek Road (Forest Road 33) and proceed north eight more miles. At that point, you will see Stein's Pillar towering over 350 feet into the air, well above the surrounding pine trees. It is plainly visible on the east side of Mill Creek Road, and the short side trip is well worth the time and effort. Be sure to stop and closely examine the remarkable landmark. It is interesting to see its unusual structure and to contemplate what volcanic events, so many years ago, caused such a structure to be there.

Stein's Pillar (courtesy of Oregon Tourism Commission)

STEINS PILLAR

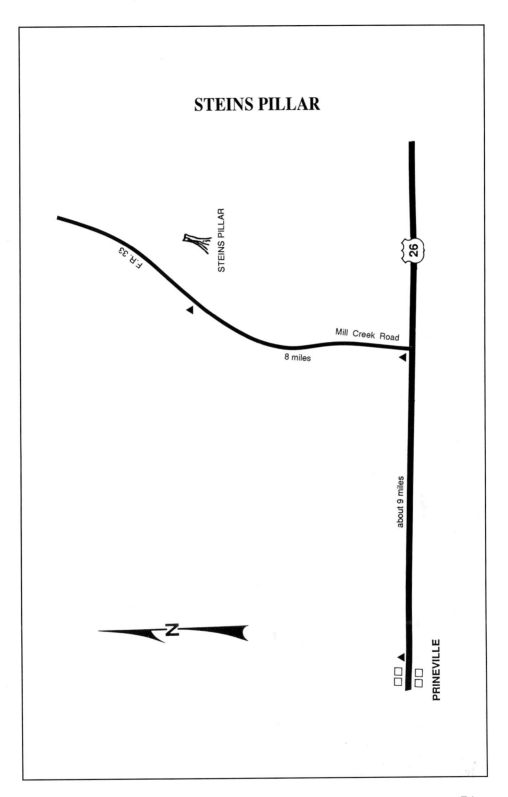

F.R. 33

STEINS PILLAR

Mill Creek Road

8 miles

US 26

about 9 miles

N

PRINEVILLE

Eagle Peak is well known for its fine moss, dendritic and angel wing agate. Up-to-date information about this and other nearby sites is available at the Prineville - Crook County Chamber of Commerce, located at 390 N. Fairview Street, in Prineville (541) 447-6304.

To get to this well-known location, it is essential that you be attentive to the given mileage to get on the correct road to the diggings when heading toward Paulina. Take the second dirt road past Eagle Rock heading off to the right. The final stretch is rough and quite steep. Rugged vehicles are essential to make it to the agate seams. If you have any doubts about being able to drive, it is advisable to simply park and hike along the road. As you approach the site, approximately one mile after leaving the pavement, diggings left by previous collectors will be seen, primarily at the base of the rim. Be sure to explore as many excavations as possible to accurately ascertain what is found at each. This will help you decide where to start.

Removing the seam agate from the tough host rhyolite requires lots of hard work and proper tools, including gads, chisels, sledge hammer, gloves and a good pair of goggles. If you don't feel like attacking the mountain with hard rock tools, there is beautiful material scattered throughout the terrain below the excavations and extending all the way to the lowlands. The digging area is extensive and the float covered lower regions are seemingly limitless. This is one of those spots where the quantity of what can be found is great. Sufficient time should be allocated to sort out only the best the site has to offer.

Eagle Peak

EAGLE PEAK

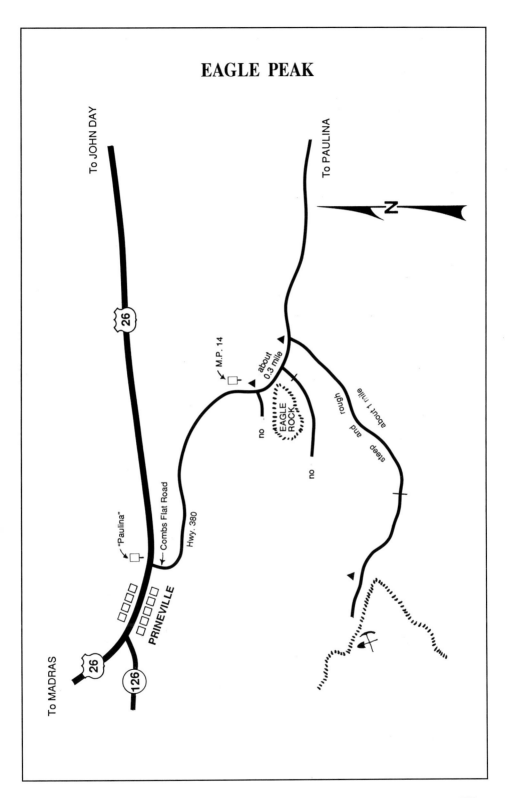

When rockhounds from Oregon hear stories of red, green and yellow moss agate, they usually conjure visions of lofty Maury Mountain and its beautiful cutting material. The Maury Mountain moss agate deposit is one of many claims maintained by the Prineville - Crook County Chamber of Commerce for use by amateur rockhounds. No fee is charged to collect there and what can be found is often striking, and filled with beautiful, contrasting internal moss inclusions. Up-to-date information about this and other nearby sites is available at the Prineville - Crook County Chamber of Commerce, located at 390 N. Fairview Street, in Prineville (541) 447-6304.

To get there, take Highway 380 (Prineville Road) to milepost 33. Just past the milepost, turn onto Forest Road 16 and continue to Forest Road 1680, four and two-tenths miles from the highway. Go right another one and one-half miles and then right at Forest Road 1690. Continue just over one-half mile to the edge of the digging area. The roads are well graded and should present no problem. There are Forest Service signs along the way giving mileage. A small parking area above the diggings even has an outhouse that has been generously supplied by the Chamber of Commerce.

The excavations are on the slopes, just beyond where you park. The best and largest chunks of agate are generally obtained with pick and shovel. The soil is relatively soft, and most of the rock you encounter will be agate. Split a portion off any suspect stone to determine its type. A small container of water is helpful for wetting freshly exposed surfaces to give better indications of quality. If you run into one of the primary agate seams, gads, chisels and a sledge hammer are necessary for breaking off sections. The work is tough, but the rewards are often great.

If you don't feel like digging or attacking the seams, there is still plenty of high-quality agate strewn throughout the hills. These pieces tend to be a little smaller than what can be procured by digging, but gem quality, fist-sized pieces are not at all uncommon. Areas about one hundred yards

or more down the slopes from the main parking lot often provide the better and larger material, but fine specimens can be found just about anywhere within the boundaries of the claim.

View from collection site

MAURY MOUNTAIN

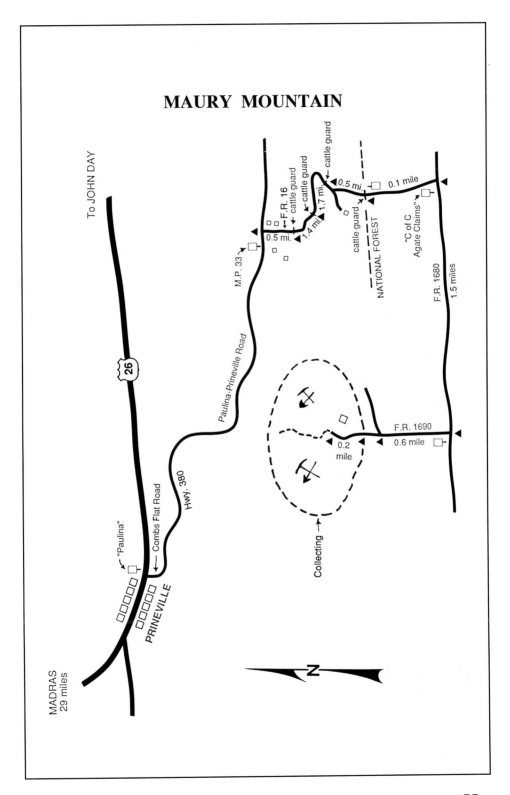

To JOHN DAY

cattle guard

cattle guard

cattle guard

F.R. 16

cattle guard

0.5 mi.

0.1 mile

1.7 mi.

1.4 mi.

cattle guard

0.5 mi.

"C of C
Agate Claims"

M.P. 33

NATIONAL FOREST

F.R. 1680

1.5 miles

Paulina-Prineville Road

F.R. 1690

0.6 mile

0.2
mile

Collecting

Hwy. 380

Combs Flat Road

"Paulina"

PRINEVILLE

MADRAS
29 miles

26

N

The two sites illustrated on the accompanying map offer the rockhound a chance to gather nodules, agate and thundereggs. This should probably be better referred to as a collecting region, rather than a collecting site, with one particular exception near Whistler Springs. To get to Site "A," go thirty-three miles east from Prineville to milepost 49. Continue three-tenths of a mile and turn left onto Forest Road 27. Go one and three-tenths miles, bear right onto Forest Road 2730 and continue another six miles to where Forest Road 2735 intersects on the right. The entire region bounded by Forest Road 2730, continuing at least six more miles, and Forest Road 2735, extending at least three miles, offers good potential for finding nodules, jasper, and agate, including some very nice moss agate.

The only way to search here is to park randomly and hike among the trees looking for traces of the jasper, agate, and occasional nodule. If you find a region of especially good concentration, it might be a good idea to do a little pick and shovel work. Since this locality has been well known for such a long time, much of the surface material near the roads has been picked up. Look for places where previous rockhounds have been digging for further clues.

Site "B" boasts agate and jasper filled thundereggs, it being a portion of the famed Whistler Springs location. A large part of this once renown rockhounding site is now within the boundaries of the Mill Creek Wilderness and there is absolutely no collecting allowed. To get to the somewhat productive open area, follow the instructions on the map, bear left onto Forest Road 200 and wind your way back to where it intersects Forest Road 27. Cross Forest Road 27 to Whistler Springs, just before reaching the Wilderness boundary.

It is necessary to do some digging with a pick and shovel. Look for places previous rockhounds have carried out their excavations and search for chips and pieces. Much of the deposit has been cleaned out, but there are still thundereggs left for anyone willing to do some work. Allow enough time to do the job properly.

There is a private agate claim a short distance farther south, just off Forest Road 27, and Highway 26 can be accessed by continuing about six more miles. This route is a little rougher and steeper than the road passing Site "A," and if you do not have a rugged vehicle, it may be a good idea to return the same way you came in.

WHISTLER SPRING

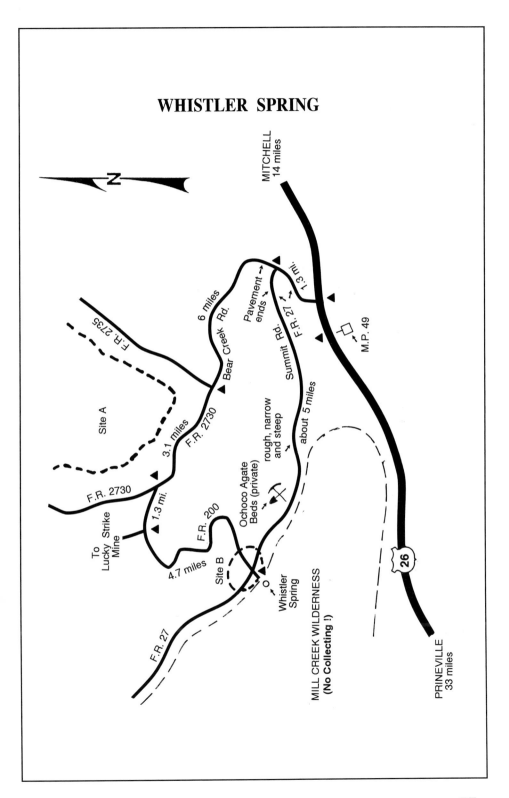

N

MITCHELL
14 miles

Pavement ends →

1.3 mi.

6 miles

F.R. 2735

Bear Creek Rd.

Summit Rd.

F.R. 27

M.P. 49

Site A

3.1 miles

F.R. 2730

rough, narrow
and steep

about 5 miles

F.R. 2730

Ochoco Agate
Beds (private)

1.3 mi.

To
Lucky Strike
Mine

F.R. 200

4.7 miles

Site B

Whistler
Spring

26

MILL CREEK WILDERNESS
(No Collecting !)

F.R. 27

PRINEVILLE
33 miles

Biggs picture rock is one of the most prized cutting materials to be found in Oregon. It is treasured by rockhounds worldwide for its beautiful swirls and patterns. The picture rock occurs in several locations in the general region near Biggs, but most deposits are protected by valid claims and closed to the public. One claimholder, however, allows rockhounds to work on his property for a fee. The claim is open year-round, weather permitting, and, if interested, it is suggested that you make advance arrangements by calling the owner, Sam Tsubota, at (541) 739-2870, or by writing to him at the Biggs Picture Jasper Mine, 91473 Biggs Rufus Highway, Wasco, OR 97065.

The cost, at time of publication, was $10.00 per person, per day, with the first ten pounds recovered being free, and anything beyond costing $1.00 per pound. It is an open pit operation, and Mr. Tsubota periodically clears it out with a bulldozer to expose fresh material. There is usually plenty to be found scattered amongst the boulders and rock within the mine itself. Unless you are very lucky, the best is obtained by attacking the tough vein with hard rock tools such as sledge hammers, gads and chisels. If you plan to work the seam directly, you should have a good pair of gloves and goggles. Tools can be borrowed, if you don't have anything with you. The vein is about one hundred feet long and varies from two to four feet wide. Colors include white, brown and black, with occasional specimens displaying hues of lavender, pink, yellow, and/or green.

In addition to the famed picture rock, the claim has recently provided some very nice, jet black jasper which can be polished into striking cabochons and other pieces. There are also a few beautiful blue agate veins similar to those found near Holley.

The best place to meet Mr. Tsubota is either at the Biggs Motel and Trailer Park, the service station, or the cafe next to the motel, all of which he owns. To get to Biggs from Interstate 84, take exit 104 (Highway 97), as shown on the map. Dry camping is available free of charge to rockhounds and hook-up spaces are half price.

Another good source of Biggs picture jasper is Dolph's Rock Shop, located in nearby Rufus, Oregon. Collectors are no longer allowed to visit the claim associated with the shop, but excellent specimens of picture jasper can be viewed and/or purchased there. Just take the old highway from Biggs and the rock shop will be about four miles east of town. For more information, write to Dolph's Rock Shop, P.O. Box 6, Rufus, OR 97050 or call (541) 739-2816.

BIGGS PICTURE JASPER

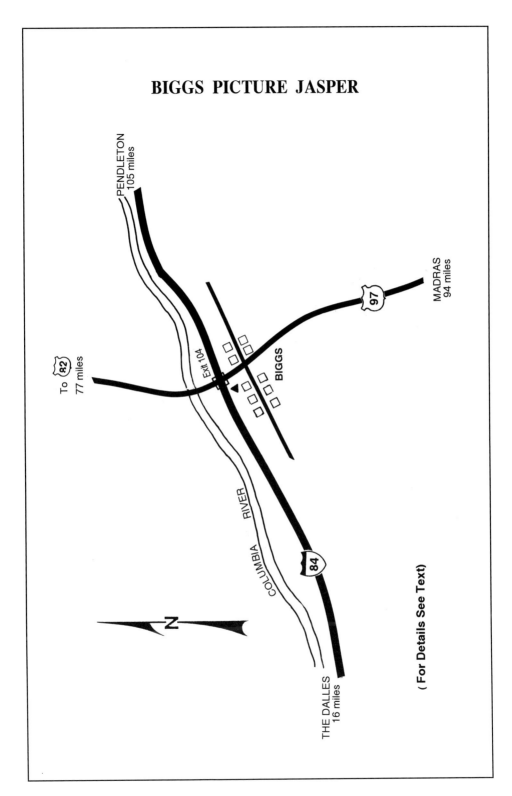

39

During the construction of Wheeler County High School, in 1949, an incredibly rich fossil deposit was unearthed. The location is still open to amateur collectors. It offers a fine opportunity to gather specimens from the renowned John Day Formation. Just about every other such John Day exposure is protected within John Day Fossil Beds National Monument or lies on inaccessible private property. Thanks to the generosity of the school, however, this spot remains open.

Simply follow the instructions provided on the accompanying map to the town of Fossil. The collecting area is next to the baseball field at the high school, and access is easy. If school is in session, be sure to check in at the main office before gathering specimens.

The town received its name from the large mammal fossils that were found at nearby Hoover Creek, but the fossils of principal interest at the high school location are primarily leaves. The John Day Formation fossils were preserved by volcanic ash deposited about 30 million years ago.

As you look through the hillside, nearly every rock will show evidence of a fossilized leaf. The best way to get complete specimens is to carefully split suspect material along a bedding plane by inserting a strong knife or chisel and gently tapping with a hammer. The host rock is somewhat soft, making it essential to protect your finds before transporting them.

Nearly thirty different species of plants have been found at this particular location. The most common species here are alder, beech, redwood, pine and maple. In addition to the leaves, one can occasionally find insects, fruits, seeds, cones and even impressions of ancient flowers. A fossilized bat and salamander have also been recovered, but such finds are very uncommon.

This is an interesting place to visit and a very productive site. Due to the generosity of the school district, collectors have been allowed to pursue their hobby without fees or unwieldy regulations and restrictions. Please always remember that this is a high school. It is essential to respect the rights of the students. Do not leave a mess or interfere with activities, otherwise the location may be closed, as have so many other fine spots.

FOSSIL

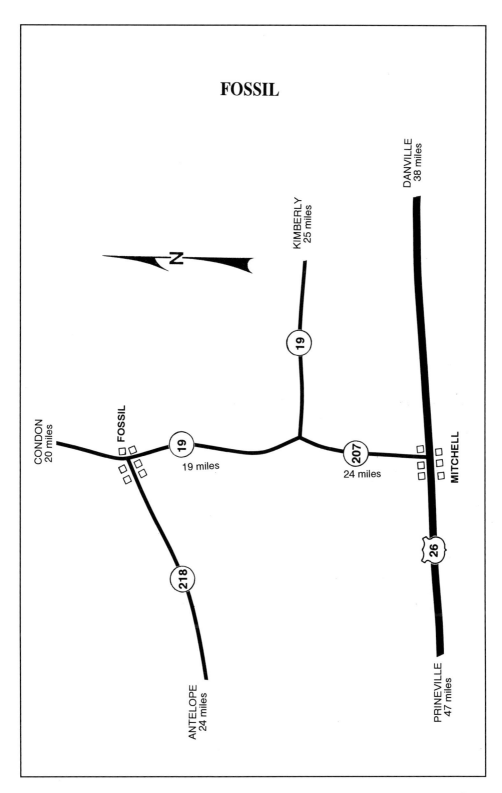

At White Fir Springs, collectors can dig for thundereggs, colorful jasper and agate. This location is protected by the Prineville - Crook County Chamber of Commerce, which is certainly one of the state's greatest supporters of amateur rockhounds. They are located at 390 N. Fairview Street, in Prineville (541) 447-6304, if you want to obtain current information.

Go east on Highway 26 approximately twenty-three miles from Prineville to milepost 41. Continue another three-tenths of a mile and turn left onto Forest Road 3350. From there, proceed on the graded dirt road four and six-tenths miles to the Chamber of Commerce sign which designates the center of the collecting site. The thundereggs occur in a rhyolite matrix with centers primarily being an agatized jasper in shades of yellow, red, brown and tan. The White Fir Springs thundereggs are highly regarded by collectors for their unusual internal patterning and color combinations. Sizes range from very small to several feet across.

Be sure to take digging tools, since it is necessary to do some excavating. Chips of the agate, jasper and broken thundereggs can frequently be found on the surface, but the best the site has to offer is underground. The soil is somewhat soft, helping to ease the work, but due to the exertion involved and the dry air, it is advisable to take plenty of extra fluids. If you don't want to do much digging, it is possible to find smaller and/or cracked thundereggs by sifting through the loose soil left by previous rockhounds surrounding pits. Nice pieces of agate and jasper can also be found. This is an enjoyable place to spend some time. Pine trees shade the digging area and the scenery is pleasant. Be advised that the spot is well known among local residents, and much work has been done here, somewhat depleting the deposit. If you are patient and willing to dig, it is still possible to find a good number of the cherished White Fir Springs thundereggs in a reasonable amount of time.

Collecting site

WHITE FIR SPRINGS

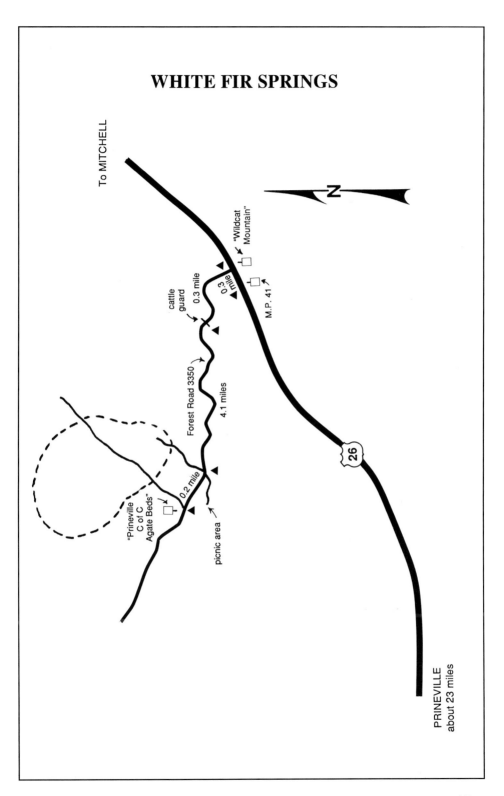

Colorful jasper, agate, and thundereggs can be found near Wildcat Mountain, about thirty miles from Prineville. Take Highway 26 twenty-three miles east from town to milepost 41. Go another three-tenths of a mile, turn left onto Forest Service Road 3350, continue five and one-half miles, turn right onto Forest Service Road 300. Proceed about one-half mile farther, and park. From that point, and continuing all the way to the Mill Creek Wilderness and the White Rock Springs Campground, rockhounds have a fairly good chance of finding jasper, agate, and thundereggs. DO NOT, under any circumstances, be tempted to dig or even remove a rock from within the boundaries of Mill Creek Wilderness. That is illegal and you could be subject to heavy fines if caught. Be satisfied with what can be gathered from the public areas. Be also advised that there are a few private claims in the region which are also closed to rockhounds.

The best way to explore this site is to park along Forest Road 300 and do a little exploration. If you don't find much at your first stop, move on a little farther and try again. Look for indications of where others have been digging. Little is left on the surface near the main roads, making it necessary to do some digging to get the larger material. You will need rock hammers, picks and shovels, as well as some luck, to get sizable pieces. Your work will be rewarded if you find some of the finest material, most notably the region's beautiful and highly prized bright orange carnelian agate or an especially nice thunderegg bearing a beautiful interior of inclusion filled agate.

This is definitely a location for the patient rockhound who is willing to do some work. Even if you don't have much luck, it is a scenic and peaceful region to spend some time. Much of the surrounding forest is respected for the fine agate and jasper that can be found just about anywhere. For that reason, if you have the time, it might be fruitful to stop just about anywhere all the way to Mill Creek Wilderness. Who knows, you may discover a completely new location.

WILDCAT MOUNTAIN

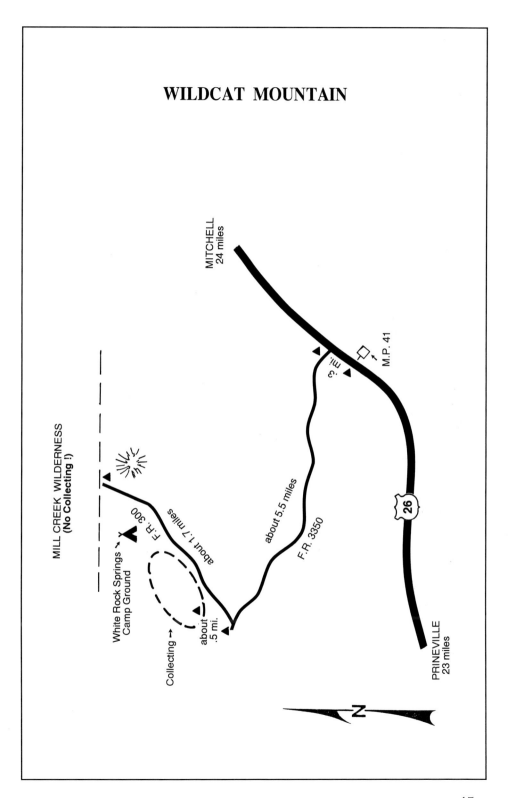

MITCHELL
24 miles

M.P. 41

.3 mi.

MILL CREEK WILDERNESS
(No Collecting !)

about 5.5 miles

F.R. 3350

26

White Rock Springs
Camp Ground

F.R. 300

about 1.7 miles

Collecting →

about
.5 mi.

PRINEVILLE
23 miles

N

One of the Prineville region's most productive thunderegg digging sites is the Lucky Strike Mine, nestled in the mountains about 40 miles northeast of town. Take Highway 26 east from Prineville to Forest Road 27, which intersects about three-tenths of a mile past milepost 49. This turnoff comes quickly, making it a good idea to slow down as you get near. The road leading off the highway to the mine is graded and well maintained. The trip is pleasant, as it winds through beautiful pine-covered scenery, interspersed with a number of spectacular overlooks.

After driving one and three-tenths miles, Forest Road 27 veers off to the left, but you should take the right fork onto Forest Road 2730. Six miles farther along, Forest Road 2735 intersects on the right. From that point, continuing along Forest Road 2730 another three miles, there are random deposits of agate on the hillside, including a very nice moss variety. Nothing is very plentiful, but if you have the time, a few stops along the way may prove to be fruitful. This is labeled Site "A" on the map.

At time of publication, the owners of the Lucky Strike Mine charged 65 cents per pound to collect, with a minimum of $3.00 required from each vehicle. The site is open from 8:00 a.m. until 5:00 p.m., starting in mid-April through October (weather permitting). It features all types of thundereggs, often filled with spectacular and colorful agate, including highly prized plume, moss, banded and layered varieties.

If you want to dig on the property, you must be supervised by one of the staff, due to insurance restrictions. For that reason, it is a good idea to make advance arrangements, just to make sure somebody will be there to provide that service. To make plans, write to the Lucky Strike Mine, P.O. Box 128, Mitchell, Oregon 97750; or call (541) 462-3332.

The digging area is periodically bulldozed to expose fresh material. It doesn't take much effort to find a number of the coveted thundereggs. Be sure to bring your own digging equipment, since it is not available for loan

at the mine. If you don't want to dig your own thundereggs, there is a virtual mountain of them to buy at main office. Free primitive camping is allowed at the Lucky Strike Mine and spring water is available.

Sign at mine entrance

LUCKY STRIKE

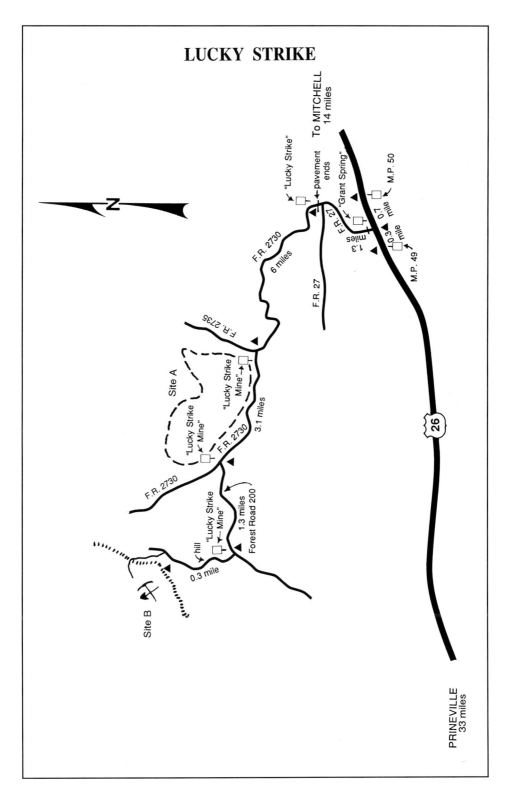

47

This location is not a specific spot, but simply the terrain alongside a stretch of highway that has a fairly good concentration of agate. To get there, take Highway 26 east from Prineville about nineteen miles to milepost 37. From there, and extending at least another five miles, the little creek just south of the road and any accessible road cuts comprise the collecting site.

If you choose to stop, be very careful and pull your vehicle well off the pavement. Cars and trucks move fast through here and are not expecting to see a pedestrian. For the same reason, do not slow below the normal flow of traffic as you search for the site or a good place to pull off. In order to maintain a safe speed, it may be necessary to actually pass through, look for a good parking place, and then double back.

The agate seems to be emanating from deposits exposed during the highway's construction. Carefully examine any of the road cuts, on either side of the pavement within the given mileage, for agate seams. Pay particular attention to the rubble at the base of such road cuts for material that has been weathered away. If you are not satisfied, you may want to attack the seams with hard rock tools such as gads, chisels and hammers. If you choose to engage in such labor, which probably won't be necessary, be very careful not to let anything roll onto the highway and do not climb onto the banks, since much of the rock is unstable.

Probably the best way to explore this location is to start near milepost 37 and work your way east, stopping as many times as you safely can do so. Some of the agate is quite plain, while other exhibits a pleasing translucent smoky gray hue. None is overly colorful, and inclusions are limited. Most, however, is quite solid and free of internal fractures or other deformities. It can be used to make nice, clean and elegant cabochons and faced stones.

HIGHWAY 26 AGATE

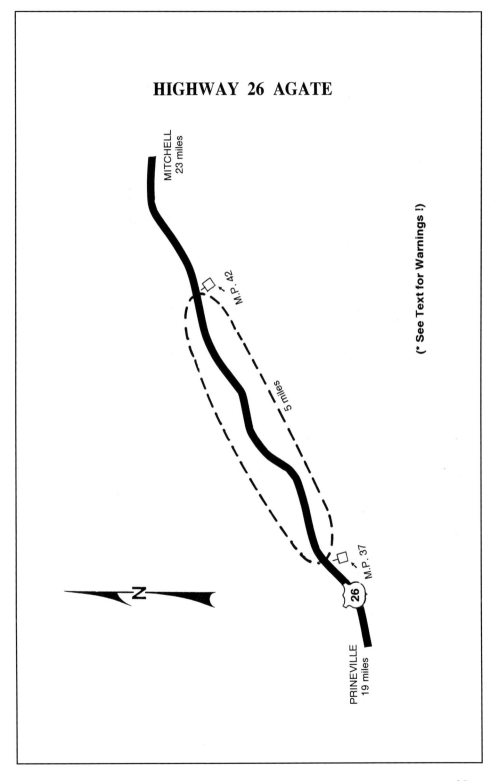

MITCHELL
23 miles

M.P. 42

5 miles

M.P. 37

26

N

PRINEVILLE
19 miles

(* See Text for Warnings !)

49

This is the well-known Prineville vistaite location, nestled within the Ochoco National Forest about twenty-eight miles east of town. Vistaite is a highly silicified form of rhyolite, appearing much like picture jasper. It generally occurs in shades of green, blue and brown. This spot has been known among Oregon rockhounds for many years. The finest material is getting harder and harder to find. If you do locate top quality specimens, even in small quantities, the trip will probably be worth the time and effort. What can be found is so nice that, at one time, a private claim governed collecting and rockhounds were allowed in only after having paid a fee. Over the years, however, the material became increasingly scarce and the claim was eventually abandoned. Unless that has changed, it is now open to anyone, and still affords an opportunity for the persistent and hard-working collector to gather some scarce but nice samples.

From Prineville, go east from town on Highway 26 to milepost 34. At that point, bear straight ahead onto Ochoco Creek Road (Forest Road 23), continuing thirteen more miles. Just after passing the ranger station, the road turns into Forest Road 22. When you reach the "Walton Lake 2 Miles" sign, go left onto Forest Road 2210 one-tenth of a mile, and then continue right one more mile on the rough tracks leading through the trees. As you approach the given mileage, look for signs of previous diggings. This marks where you should concentrate your efforts. Some material can be found as float in the black adobe, but it is scarce. Most is buried and only obtainable by using picks, pry bars and shovels.

This is not an easy collecting site and, unless you get very lucky and stumble upon a previously undiscovered deposit of this exquisite cutting material, you will have to be satisfied with only small pieces. The vistaite takes a good polish, but not high gloss. If displaying multiple colors, it can be used to make very fine lapidary items which rival the best picture material to be found anywhere.

WALTON LAKE

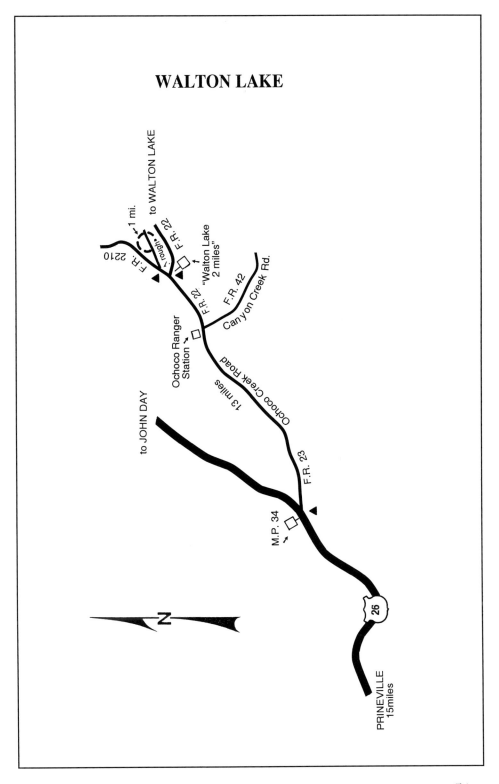

The jade-like green jasper found at this well-known Oregon rockhounding site is prized by collectors, and, for that reason, the location has been substantially depleted over the years. The agate found here ranges in color from a pale blue to an exquisite dark green. Nowadays, it takes lots of work and patience to discover the best green material, but it still can be found by those willing to spend the needed time and effort.

To get there, take Highway 26 about 30 miles east from Prineville to milepost 48 and then continue another six-tenths of a mile to Pisqah Lookout Road (Forest Service Road 2630). Go right three and two-tenths miles, turn right at Forest Road 300, travel another two miles. At that point, some ruts will be seen leading off to the right a short distance to the digging site.

Small amounts of jasper will be encountered in float, but it is necessary to do some heavy digging with pick, shovel, gads, chisel and hammer to remove the prize material from its place in the side of the mountain. To get an idea where to start, look for where earlier rockhounds have been digging. Closely examine the soil immediately surrounding any of the pits and burrows to get an idea as to what was found there. If little or nothing of interest is spotted, probably that particular pit was not too productive or has been totally worked out. In addition, it seems that digging areas nearest the road are more picked over and depleted than those in out-of-the-way places.

Be forewarned that it is common for this site to receive substantial amounts of snow during the winter, making it completely inaccessible. This is primarily a summer collecting locality. At one time, a claim was held here, and a fee charged to dig. That no longer seems to be the case, but if this has changed, respect the rights of the owners and seek permission to collect ahead of time. Current information can probably be obtained at the Prineville Chamber of Commerce 390 N. Fairview St., Prineville (541) 447-6304 or at any rock shop in town.

MITCHELL

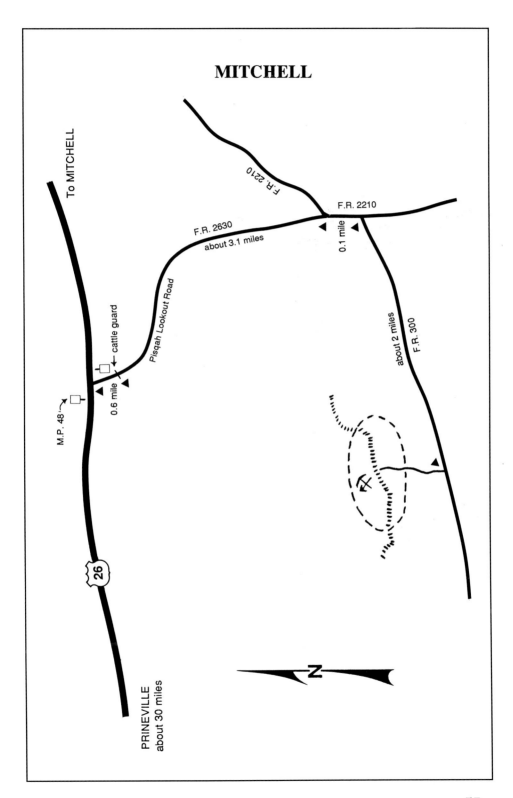

To MITCHELL

F.R. 2210

F.R. 2630
about 3.1 miles

F.R. 2210
0.1 mile

Pisqah Lookout Road

cattle guard

about 2 miles
F.R. 300

M.P. 48

0.6 mile

26

N

PRINEVILLE
about 30 miles

The John Day Fossil Beds offer an opportunity to see one of the nation's premier fossil localities and some of Oregon's most unusual scenery. It is composed of three distinct units, all situated in the same general area, but COLLECTING IS NOT ALLOWED! In spite of the collecting restriction, however, it still makes a most interesting side trip.

The area was first determined to be of great scientific value in the mid-1800s by a pioneer minister named Thomas Condon. Many of the fossils that have been found throughout the John Day Valley are over 55 million years old and represent life that inhabited the region when it was a jungle and, more recently, savanna and thick woodlands. Within the boundaries of the National Monument is the Clarno Nut Beds which have provided researchers some of the best examples of fossil plant-life. The remains of countless ancient animals have also been unearthed over the years. Many of these animals are now extinct, and some found nowhere else. The list includes brontotheres, amynodonts, hyaenadonts, rhinos, tapirs, cats, horses, camels, pigs, rodents, deer, bear, weasels, dogs, just to name a few.

The Park's main exhibit area is at Sheep Rock, three miles north of U.S. Highway 26, on State Highway 19. It is open daily from 8:30 a.m. until 6:00 p.m., from mid-March through October. Within its boundaries are the Blue Basin hiking trail, the fossil examination laboratory, and Sheep Rock, a massive and colorful outcrop of the John Day Formation. At the Painted Hills Unit, an information station is located in the picnic area and a short drive farther is the spectacular Painted Hills Overlook. There are also three hiking trails through some more remote portions of the Monument. At Clarno Unit, information is posted on a bulletin board in the picnic area. For more information, write to Superintendent, John Day Fossil Beds National Monument, H.R.C. 82, Box 126, Kimberly, OR 97848, or call (541) 987-2333.

Visitor center

JOHN DAY FOSSIL BEDS

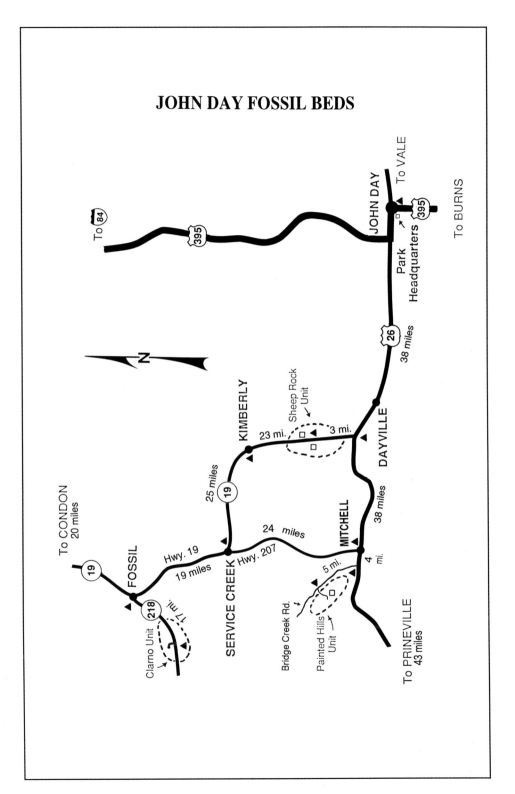

Petrified wood can be found throughout the region just north of Bates. Be advised, however, that most is not of high quality. In fact, lots of it is very uninteresting, but a trip through this scenic area provides a setting for some enjoyable exploration. To get to Bates, go one mile north on Highway 7 from where it intersects Highway 26, about fifteen miles east of Prairie City. At that point is Susanville Road, and it is there where you should turn left, as shown on the map. About six-tenths of a mile from Highway 7 is a road cut where you can find a very interesting "wormhole" rock which can be used for interesting display pieces.

Some wood can be found in the region adjacent to that road cut, but the best hunting areas are accessed by taking any of the roads illustrated on the map. Just drive a short distance into the hills on Forest Road 2055, Forest Road 2010, or Vinegar Creek Road, and, wherever you spot a clearing or region of erosion, pull off and inspect it. There is no specific location where the wood is most prevalent and a lot of luck is involved.

Be sure to carefully examine any rock you encounter, since some of it might be wood. Much of what can be found at this locality tends to be severely eroded or broken up in such a way that identification is not as easy as it might be. In addition, the colors tend to be rather plain, in shades of gray, brown and even black. Once you find a few pieces, subsequent material will be easier to find, since your eyes will have been "trained" to spot it.

Don't be discouraged if you do not find much surface material. Have patience, and you surely will stumble upon chunks that are quite nice and capable of taking a high-gloss polish. Perseverance and a willingness to spend time for adequate exploration are the key factors needed for success. Look through the numerous dredge tailings that you might stumble upon, many not only contain petrified wood, but potentially colorful and inclusion

 filled agate and jasper.

View of road cut just off Highway 7

BATES

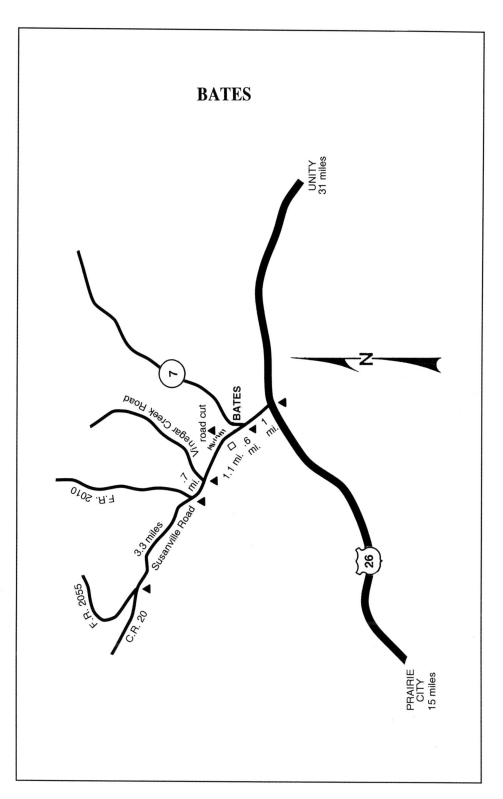

UNITY
31 miles

N

7

BATES

road cut

Vinegar Creek Road

.7 mi.

F.R. 2010

3.3 miles

Susanville Road

F.R. 2055

C.R. 20

1.1 mi.

.6 mi.

1 mi.

26

PRAIRIE CITY
15 miles

This location offers rockhounds a variety of interesting minerals. The collecting is worthwhile, the scenery is nice and the visit provides an enjoyable trip into Oregon's past. To gain access to Site "A," go about ten miles east from Bates on Highway 7 to the Greenhorn turnoff. Go north six and eight-tenths miles to the series of road cuts. Pull off the main roadway and explore the cuts and the rubble below for specimens of serpentine. There are exhibits of nice deep jade-like green color, but most is dark, being almost black. The material tends to be flaky, but some is solid enough to be carved or shaped into cabochons and polished pieces. There is some nondescript petrified wood throughout the terrain surrounding the road cuts.

After sampling several spots at Site "A," continue to the intersection, as shown on the map. From there, go left and drive approximately two miles to where tracks can be seen leading in from the right. This marks the center of Site "B" and offers an opportunity to gather some interesting mineral and fossil specimens. Much of the gravel in this part of Oregon was deposited by gold dredges. It is within those tailings and along the many streams that collectors can find, among other things, petrified wood, serpentine, jasper, chert, and tiny fossilized fern stems. Most is somewhat small, but occasional fist-size chunks can also be found.

Be sure to continue to Greenhorn, two-tenths of a mile farther along Forest Service Road 1042. Greenhorn is the smallest and highest incorporated town in Oregon, situated at 6,500 feet above sea level. Nothing much remains, but at one time, over 500 people lived there, supporting thousands of prospectors. The town dates back to the 1870s and the Greenhorn Gold Mine was in operation until 1925. Doubling back on Forest Service Road 1042 will take you to what remains of the once prosperous town of Granite. It owed its existence to gold being found on nearby Granite Creek in 1862. Many of the old stores, and the cemetery, still remain.

GREENHORN

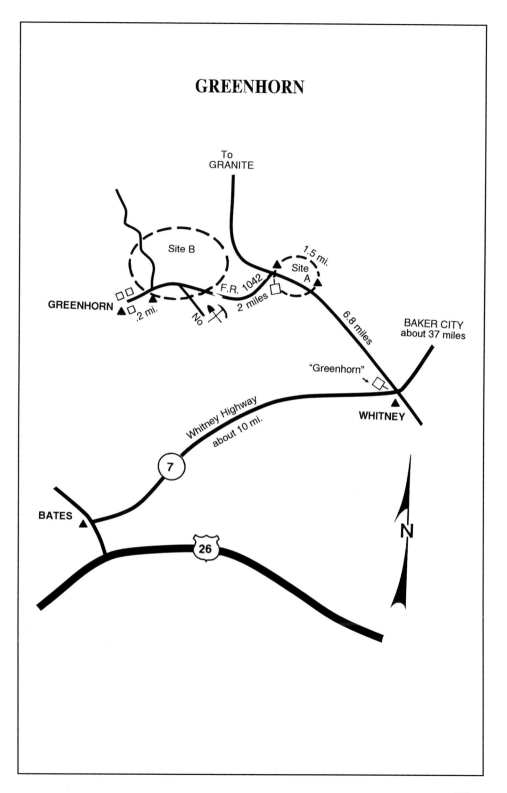

To
GRANITE

Site B

1.5 mi.

Site
A

F.R. 1042

GREENHORN

.2 mi.

No

2 miles

6.8 miles

BAKER CITY
about 37 miles

"Greenhorn"

WHITNEY

Whitney Highway
about 10 mi.

7

BATES

26

N

Three locations offer amateur prospectors a legitimate chance for finding gold with a pan, sluice or small dredge. They are situated within the Wallowa-Whitman National Forest in an area generally regarded as Oregon's premier gold-producing region. Because of its popularity, the Wallowa-Whitman National Forest is packed with private claims, and amateurs must not trespass onto such protected areas. The sites mentioned here have been set aside for general public use and recreational prospecting is permitted within their boundaries.

To get to Site "A," go west on Highway 7 from Baker City approximately twenty-one miles. From there, turn right onto Forest Road 7240, continue three and four-tenths miles, turn left onto Forest Road 6510 another nine-tenths of a mile. Turn left again onto Forest Road 6530 and go one and two-tenths more miles to the Deer Creek Campground. Within the borders of that recreational area, you can try your luck at finding gold anywhere along the creek.

Site "B" is reached by returning to Highway 7 and continuing west three and three-tenths miles to Sumpter Junction. Turn right and continue two and nine-tenths miles to the old town of Sumpter, which is an interesting place to spend some time. It was first settled in 1862 and was named after Fort Sumpter in South Carolina. At its prime, Sumpter boasted over 4,000 inhabitants and was the center of the region's gold mining activity. Be sure to stop at the restored gold dredge near the south side of town. Seeing the colossal dredge is interesting and the visitor center offers good information about the region's history.

Pass through Sumpter and drive another two and eight-tenths miles to McCully Forks Campground. As before, all streams within the campground boundaries are open to recreational gold panning, sluicing or dredging.

Site "C" is accessed nine miles farther west from Sumpter Junction along Highway 7. Turn left at the old town of Whitney onto County Road 529. Go two and two-tenths miles to the Antlers Forest Service Station and try your luck at finding gold in this public access portion of the Burnt River.

Each of these locations is respected for the gold that can still be found, but as is the case with any precious mineral, don't expect to find huge nuggets or color in every pan. It takes patience to find much, but the scenery is beautiful, the historic areas fascinating, and the gold is there. Be also advised, if planning to use a dredge, an Oregon State Permit is required. Ask for the NPDES, 0700-J permit for recreational dredges with up to a 4-inch nozzle size. It is available from the Oregon Department of Environmental Quality, 811 SW Sixth Avenue, Portland, OR 97204. Additional information about these sites can be obtained from the Forest Supervisor, P.O. Box 907, Baker City, OR 97814, (503) 523-6391.

SUMPTER

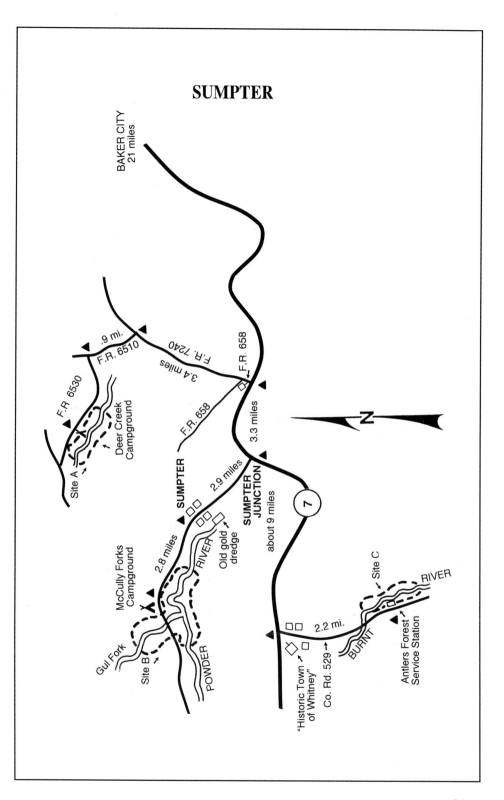

These three sites encompass extensive territory and afford an opportunity to find everything from gold to petrified wood, agate, jasper and even geodes. Site "A" is noted for its nice jade-like green jasper. Start by taking Exit 327 from Interstate 84, at Durkee. Double back on Old Highway 30 about four miles to Shirttail Creek Road. Turn right and stop randomly along Shirttail Creek, carefully inspecting the rocks in and around the waterway. Be certain not to trespass onto private land. Restrict all collecting to open public areas. Farther south, near Huntington, large geodes have been reportedly found, but the author has not yet had an opportunity to do any collecting there. Local inquiry will be necessary to get more specific information.

The widespread region alongside Highway 86, between Baker City and Richland, especially to the south, offers top quality quartz gemstones, including agate, in every imaginable hue and pattern, vividly colored jasper, chalcedony, and even some petrified wood. This vast forty-two-mile-long region is designated as Site "B" and, as was the case at Shirttail Creek, there is an abundance of private property throughout the area. Don't enter such lands without first gaining permission. Material is scattered, with some spots far more productive than others. If you don't find much at your first stop, simply move a little farther down the road and try again.

Site "C" is a noted gold-producing region. Be advised that private claims are scattered throughout the area, but the Forest Service has set aside one fairly productive panning, sluicing and dredging location for the general public. It is Eagle Forks Campground. To get there from Richland, take Newbridge Road north from town about nine miles. Newbridge Road turns into Forest Service Road 7735 once it enters the forest.

As is the case at most public access gold localities, don't expect to find huge nuggets or color in every pan. You can prospect anywhere within the campground boundaries and it is a scenic and relaxing place to spend some time. Sudden wealth, however, is not guaranteed. If you want to use a recreational dredge at Eagle Forks, an Oregon State Permit is required. Ask for the NPDES, 0700-J permit for recreational dredges up to a 4-inch nozzle size. It is available from the Oregon Department of Environmental Quality, 811 SW Sixth Avenue, Portland, OR 97204. Additional information can be obtained from the Forest Supervisor, P.O. Box 907, Baker City, OR 97814, (541) 523-6391.

BAKER CITY

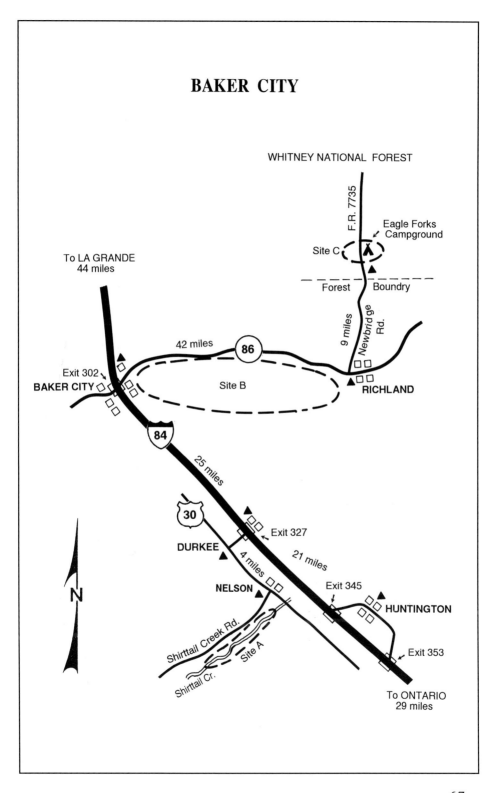

WHITNEY NATIONAL FOREST

F.R. 7735

Eagle Forks
Campground

Site C

Forest   Boundry

To LA GRANDE
44 miles

9 miles

Newbridge Rd.

42 miles 86

Exit 302
BAKER CITY

Site B

RICHLAND

84

25 miles

30

Exit 327

DURKEE

4 miles

21 miles

NELSON

Exit 345

HUNTINGTON

N

Shirttail Creek Rd.

Site A

Shirttail Cr.

Exit 353

To ONTARIO
29 miles

There are only two places in the entire world where almandine star garnets can be found. One is in India and the other is at Emerald Creek, Idaho. Even though it is not in Oregon, it is close, and is such an important spot that it should be mentioned. The stars are caused by tiny needles of rutile embedded in the garnet, which line up with the interior crystal structure. If the needles are oriented in two directions, four rays are produced and if lined up in three directions, a very rare-six ray variety is formed.

This site is operated by the U. S. Forest Service. At time of publication, a daily collecting fee of $10.00 per adult and $5.00 per child under 14 was charged. There is a five pound per day limit, but you can purchase a second permit for each additional five pounds or fraction. The limit is 30 pounds of garnet per year. Permits are required for removal of garnets by anyone digging, screening or washing the gravel. Work is restricted to designated areas. Emerald Creek is open the Saturday of Memorial Day weekend through the Tuesday after Labor Day, from 8:00 a.m. until 5:00 p.m.

Rockhounds must provide their own non-motorized digging equipment and the Forest Service suggests rubber boots, change of clothes, a round-point shovel, a pick, a bucket, a one-fourth-inch wire mesh screening box, and a container for storing the garnets. Crystal sizes range from nearly microscopic to occasional "giants" as large as an orange. To recover them, first remove between one and ten feet of overburden and then scoop the garnet-bearing soil, which is directly above the schist bedrock, into a screen for washing, sorting, and collecting, always looking for sizable crystals. Also, chunks of the garnet bearing schist can be used to make great display pieces. For more information write to the District Ranger, St. Joe Ranger District, P.O. Box 407, ID 83861 or call (208) 245-2531.

A split, six ray star garnet (rare)

EMERALD CREEK

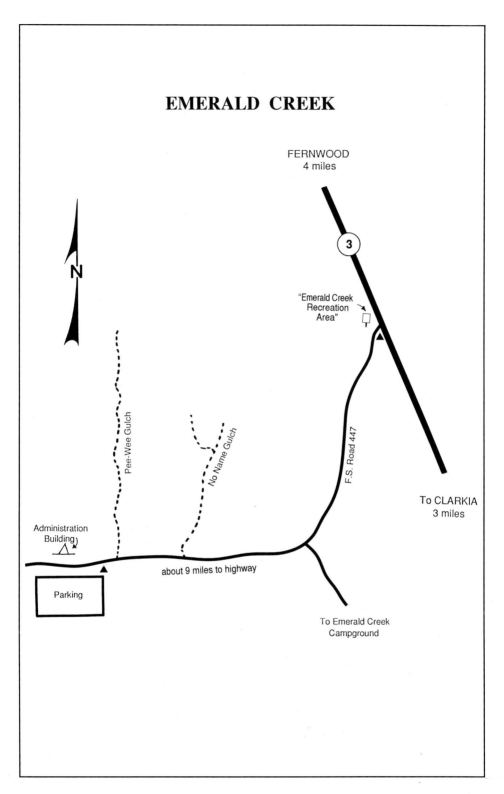

FERNWOOD
4 miles

N

③

"Emerald Creek
Recreation
Area"

F.S. Road 447

Pee-Wee Gulch

No Name Gulch

To CLARKIA
3 miles

Administration
Building

Parking

about 9 miles to highway

To Emerald Creek
Campground

This location offers the collector a variety of quality minerals. The material of primary interest is the renown Hog Creek moss agate, but one can also pick up clear agate, paisley agate, nice multi-colored agate, occasional pieces of plume agate, oolitic agate, chunks of brightly colored jasper, rhyolite, nodules, and white or light blue chalcedony roses.

To get there, go west three and one-half miles on Highway 70 from where it intersects Highway 95 Spur. At that point, turn north onto Jonathan Road and continue just over eight miles to Hog Creek and the center of the collecting site. Look for the cement stairs, which are partially obstructed by brush, as a landmark to help identify the collecting area.

From the creek, material can be found in just about every direction, especially in the eroded areas on the west and in the tiny canyon leading northeast from the road. Agate, jasper and chalcedony can be picked up on either side of Hog Creek for quite a distance. Be warned that nothing will be found in huge quantities. There is enough, however, to reward a patient and persistent rockhound with acceptable amounts of fine specimens. Digging in the soft soil is often helpful, but, if you do dig, be sure to fill in the holes to prevent injury to grazing cattle.

The rhyolite and nodules are found in the little canyon leading northeast from the road. Look in the rubble below the canyon walls or dig into the embankments directly. If you do any excavating, though, be very careful not to knock anything down onto others.

WEISER-AGATE AND JASPER

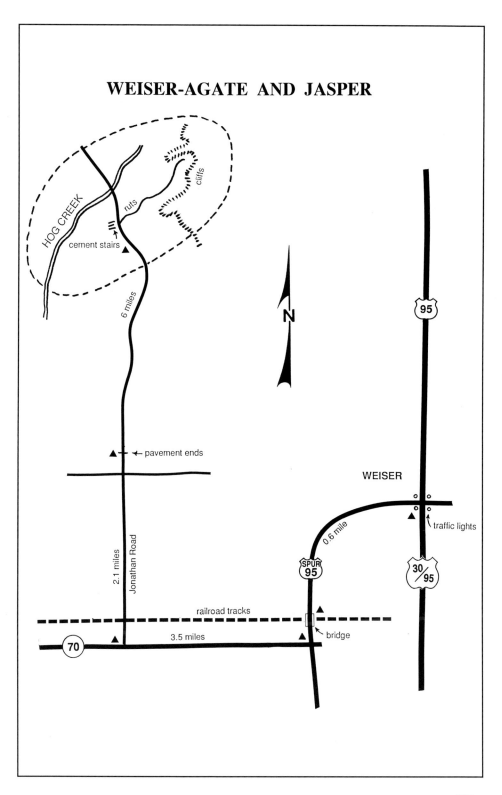

HOG CREEK

cliffs

ruts

cement stairs

6 miles

pavement ends

N

WEISER

95

0.6 mile

traffic lights

2.1 miles

Jonathan Road

SPUR
95

30/95

railroad tracks

bridge

70

3.5 miles

The fine plume and moss agate found near Graveyard Point is renowned the world over. While most of the collecting is in Oregon, access is from Highway 95 in Idaho, two and eight-tenths miles south of Homedale. Follow Graveyard Point Road west four and eight-tenths miles to where a footbridge can be seen crossing the canal on the left.

The trail leading from the footbridge up the side of the hill goes to Site "A." Park well off the main road, walk across the bridge, and hike along the trail to the agate outcrops. It is advisable to sample different portions of the extensive deposit to get a good idea of the different variations of agate.

Once you have decided which section of the outcrop you want to work on, it is necessary to use hard rock equipment, including a sledge hammer, chisels, pry bar and gads to remove pieces of the precious mineral from its place on the mountain. If that doesn't appeal to you, there is plenty of fine, but generally small, chunks of the agate lying all over the ground below the diggings. Many rockhounds are very satisfied with what can be picked up in this manner, avoiding the tough hammer and chisel work.

To get to Site "B," you must first cross the canal. There is a bridge two and eight-tenths miles farther west and another back to the north. Due to recent bad weather in the region, be certain the bridge you choose to cross on is stable, since there have been some washouts over the years.

Whichever access you use, Site "B" boasts good quality moss agate, which is found in float. Simply walk through the brush and soft soil to obtain good specimens. The colors don't seem to be as vivid as at Site "A" or as varied, but excellent material can be picked up. Much is clear with fine black and red inclusions. This field is extensive, so try any or all the roads leading through it. At Site "C," collectors can find beautiful plume and moss agate. You will spot diggings similar to those at Site "A," designating where

to stop. Be advised, there are some gem claims in the area. You should not violate the rights of the claim holders. There is plenty to be found in the surrounding, public areas.

Crossing the bridge on the way to Site "A"

GRAVEYARD POINT

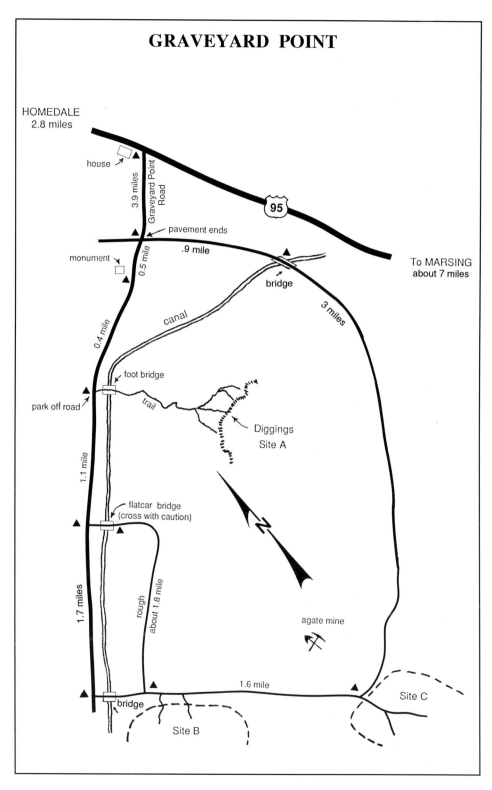

HOMEDALE
2.8 miles

house

3.9 miles

Graveyard Point Road

95

pavement ends

.9 mile

monument

0.5 mile

To MARSING
about 7 miles

bridge

3 miles

canal

0.4 mile

foot bridge

trail

park off road

Diggings
Site A

1.1 mile

flatcar bridge
(cross with caution)

1.7 miles

rough

about 1.8 mile

agate mine

1.6 mile

Site C

bridge

Site B

This region, at one time, afforded rockhounds an abundance of very nice obsidian and Apache tears. It now is one of the nation's newest National Monuments and completely closed to collecting. The area is still of great interest to anyone wanting to know more about the geology of the Northwest, particularly volcanoes. It is worth taking some time to explore.

Within the Monument is Lava Cast Forest, featuring lava "trees," casts, and molds which were created about 7,000 years ago when an entire forest was engulfed by molten lava leaving behind the now empty voids where the wood long ago disintegrated away. There are numerous lava caves open for exploration, massive lava flows, tons of pumice and obsidian, and spectacular scenery. This is a result of volcanic activity that started approximately 700,000 years ago and continued, sporadically, until about 650 A.D.

On the slopes of prominent Newberry Volcano are over 400 cinder cones, resulting from the many eruptions that have taken place over the centuries. At the top is massive Newberry Crater, four miles across and encompassing approximately seventeen square miles. While traveling through Newberry National Monument, you will be able to see many of the massive and ruggedly beautiful lava flows which permeate the region, looking like great tongues of tar. Be sure to stop at the Lava Lands Visitor Center for more information about the many sights within the Monument. It is situated about eleven miles south of Bend, just off Highway 97. Take sufficient time to explore as much of the region as possible. To do so will give you a much better understanding of the immensely powerful geological actions that helped form the rugged terrain so prevalent in this part of the world.

View of Newberry caldera, looking south (courtesy of Oregon Dept. of Geology and Mineral Industries)

NEWBERRY NATIONAL VOLCANIC MONUMENT

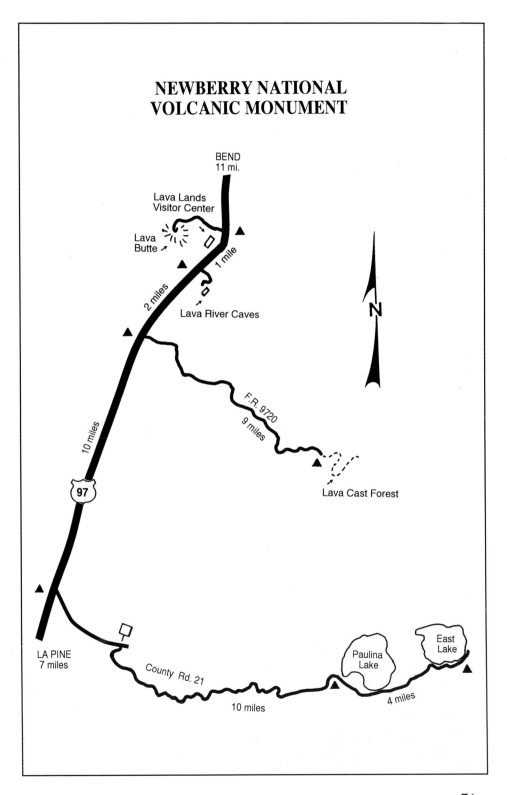

BEND
11 mi.

Lava Lands
Visitor Center

Lava
Butte

1 mile

2 miles

Lava River Caves

N

F.R. 9720
9 miles

Lava Cast Forest

10 miles

97

LA PINE
7 miles

County Rd. 21

10 miles

Paulina
Lake

East
Lake

4 miles

Plenty of agate, jasper, chalcedony and carnelian can be found throughout gravel deposits along a three-mile stretch of the North Umpqua River between the towns of Glide and Idleyld Park. In addition, interesting petrified wood, sometimes containing unusual worm holes, can be procured.

To reach this scenic and relaxing locality, take Exit 124 from Interstate 5 and go northeast on Highway 138 approximately seventeen miles to the small town of Glide. Just beyond Glide, the road passes over the North Umpqua, and continues three miles to Idleyld Park. The river is relatively close to the roadway. Find an open access to the river and examine the gravel and rock for the collectibles.

Rockhounding at this location is best accomplished during the summer months when the water is low. This allows for the formation of gem-bearing gravel bars which trap the agate, jasper, chalcedony and wood. Some of the material found here is quite colorful and frequently contains fascinating inclusions.

The North Umpqua River is a potentially powerful waterway. It is advisable not to do any wading. Be satisfied with what can be easily reached along the shore or within safely accessed gravel bars. In addition, note that there is private property along the river. You should never trespass without first gaining permission to do so. Local inquiry is helpful to determine best access to public areas along the river.

As happens with any river gravel collecting, don't forget that river rock is usually very abraded and difficult to identify and, when dry, most appear to be dull and uninteresting. Look for faint coloration and split any such stones to show a fresh, unabraded surface to evaluate the true potential.

UMPQUA RIVER

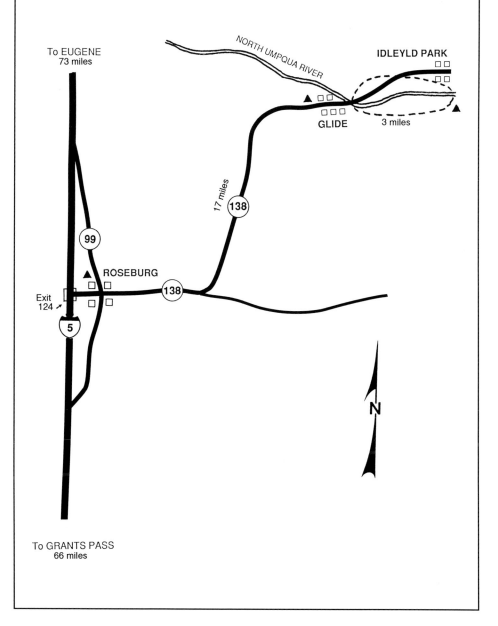

To EUGENE
73 miles

NORTH UMPQUA RIVER

IDLEYLD PARK

GLIDE

3 miles

17 miles

138

99

ROSEBURG

138

Exit
124

5

N

To GRANTS PASS
66 miles

The Rogue River cuts a picturesque canyon through native rock near the little town of Agness. Within gravel bars and upon banks of the river stretching for miles in either direction from town, rockhounds can often find beautiful specimens of agate, jasper, chalcedony, carnelian and grossularite garnet. This locality is not only productive, from a rockhounding point of view, but is also a very picturesque location.

To get there, go north on Highway 101 from Gold Beach, approximately two miles. Just before crossing the bridge spanning the Rogue River, County Road 595 intersects on the right. Turn and follow that scenic route into the National Forest and to Agness, a total of about twenty-eight miles.

As was mentioned in previous descriptions of river collecting, rockhounding is best accomplished during the summer months when the water level is low. This enables the formation of gravel bars which trap rock being carried by the river, including the colorful agate, jasper, chalcedony, carnelian and garnet. Even when the water level is low, however, the Rogue River is a mighty waterway. Do not even consider wading into its strong currents. Be satisfied with what you can gather from the riverbanks or upon gravel bars emanating from the shore. There is some private property along the river near Agness and you should never trespass without first gaining permission to do so. Be sure to restrict all collecting to open areas within the Siskiyou National Forest.

As is the case with any river gravel collecting, you may be discouraged when you first start picking up specimens. Everything appears to be dull and uninteresting. Remember, though, that the abrasive actions of the current scratches the surface of all entrapped stone making it difficult to accurately ascertain the true nature of what might be concealed within its interior. Look for faint color and then split any such rock to expose a fresh, unabraded surface to evaluate the true potential.

Rouge River

AGNESS AGATE

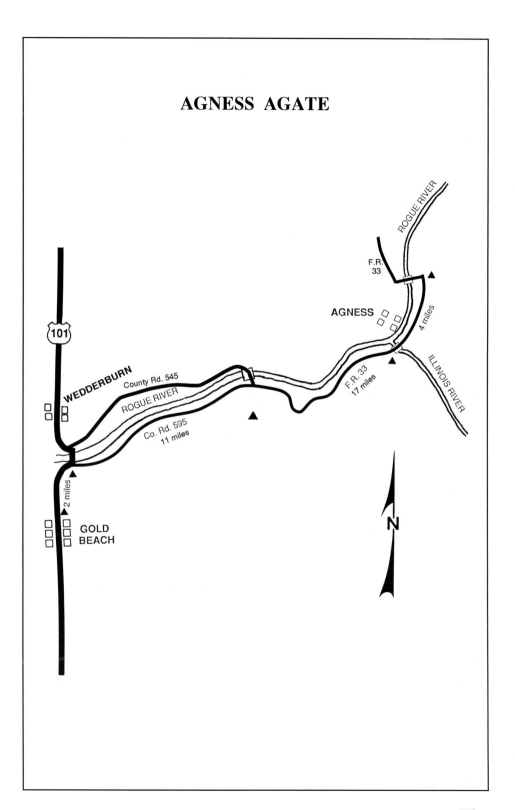

Beautiful green grossular garnet, locally referred to as "Oregon Jade," nice pink rhodonite, and vivid red jasper can all be collected in a region southwest of Oregon Caves National Monument. From Grants Pass, go southwest about thirty-seven miles on Highway 199 to Cave Junction. At that point, continue east five and one-half miles to the small town of Holland, as shown on the map. The primary mineral collecting is done along Althouse Creek, which is accessed by turning south and continuing one more mile on Althouse Creek Road to where the little waterway can be spotted on the right.

From there and extending a few more miles, the search becomes random. Find an open access to the river and examine the gravel and rock for collectibles. The best time to search is usually during the summer months when the water level is low, thereby allowing for the formation of gravel bars which trap rock being carried by the current. Inspect the banks of Althouse Creek, as well as safely reached gravel bars. Be sure to keep in mind that river rock is usually very abraded and difficult to identify. Look for faint green, pink, or red color and then split such stones to expose a fresh, unabraded surface to evaluate their true potential. In addition, look through any of the old dredging piles which can be spotted throughout the general area.

If you have time, it should be noted that the rhodonite originates in deposits higher up the hillsides toward Oregon Caves National Monument. The author has not yet been able to pinpoint their actual location, but local inquiry might provide you with some rewarding leads. There is private property throughout this region and you should be careful not to trespass without first gaining permission to do so.

Oregon Caves National Monument is NOT A COLLECTING SITE, but, it is a fascinating place to visit for anyone interested in geology. While in the area, it would be foolish not to visit. The caves themselves are worth the trip, being filled with beautiful stalactites, stalagmites and other forms of dripstone. The heavily contorted and folded marble near the parking area also provides an opportunity to view a most unusual geologic phenomenon. They are accessible by paved highway. For more information, contact Oregon Caves National Monument, P.O. Box 128, Cave Junction, OR 97523, or phone (541) 592-3400.

ALTHOUSE CREEK

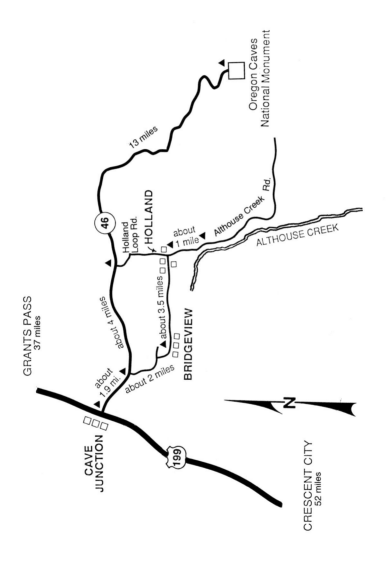

Three locations offer amateur prospectors a good likelihood for finding gold. The region is scenic and spending a few days could prove to be productive, in finding little flakes and nuggets, and also relaxing. A permit from the Applegate Ranger District is required, and it can be procured at the Ranger Station, or by writing to the Applegate Ranger District, 6941 Upper Applegate Road, Jacksonville, OR 97530, (541) 899-1812. The fees, at time of publication, were $1.00 per person, per day, to pan; $5.00 per day for dredging (maximum three-inch intake); $2.00 per day to operate a sluice, which includes panning; and $2.00 per day for using a metal detector. A valid dredging permit must also be displayed. Dredging permits can be obtained from the Oregon Department of Environmental Quality, 811 SW Sixth Avenue, Portland, OR 97204. Ask for the NPDES, 0700-J permit for recreational dredges up to a 4-inch nozzle size. The sites are open year-round, but dredging is limited from July 1 through September 15 except by waiver.

Site "A" is reached by taking the road to Applegate Reservoir two and eight-tenths miles south from Ruch. Turn left and follow Little Applegate Road ten miles to Tunnel Ridge Recreation Site and Little Applegate Recreation Site. Little Applegate River within the region encompassed by the two campgrounds is open to recreational prospectors and closed to private claims.

If you have the time and energy, hike along the Sterling Mine Trail. Here you can see portions of the massive Sterling Mine Ditch, a remnant of the enormous hydraulic mining operation conducted during the late 1800s. The ditch can be accessed from either Tunnel Ridge or Little Applegate. Complete information can be secured at the Ranger Station. To get to Site "B," continue two and seven-tenths miles south from the Ranger Station, turn left and follow Beaver Creek Road two and eight-tenths miles to Beaver-Sulphur Campground. Gold prospecting is allowed. Be advised only panning

is permitted, no dredging or sluicing. Site "C," is situated at Kanaka Gulch. Continue toward Applegate reservoir four and nine-tenths miles from Beaver Creek Road, immediately after passing over the river and just before reaching the dam, turn right onto the tough-to-spot little road heading down the hill. Note that panning and sluicing is allowed there, but no dredging.

Applegate River at
Jackson Picnic Area

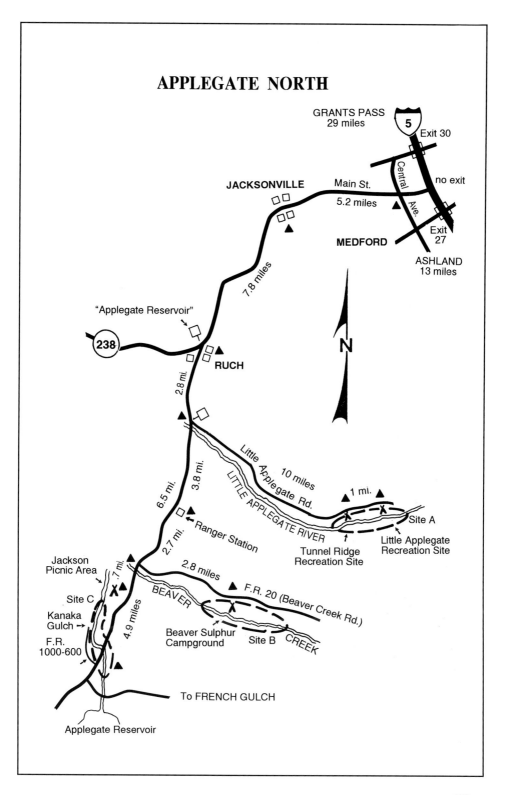

APPLEGATE NORTH

GRANTS PASS
29 miles

5

Exit 30

Central Ave.

no exit

JACKSONVILLE

Main St.
5.2 miles

MEDFORD

Exit 27

ASHLAND
13 miles

7.8 miles

"Applegate Reservoir"

238

2.8 mi.

RUCH

N

Little Applegate Rd.

LITTLE APPLEGATE RIVER

10 miles

1 mi.

Site A

Little Applegate
Recreation Site

Tunnel Ridge
Recreation Site

6.5 mi.

3.8 mi.

2.7 mi.

Ranger Station

Jackson
Picnic Area

.7 mi.

Site C

BEAVER

2.8 miles

F.R. 20 (Beaver Creek Rd.)

Kanaka
Gulch

4.9 miles

Beaver Sulphur
Campground

Site B

CREEK

F.R.
1000-600

To FRENCH GULCH

Applegate Reservoir

These five locations offer additional opportunities to find gold within one of Oregon's premier prospecting regions. Two of the sites are in Oregon, the other three are actually in California. The Oregon sites require special prospecting permits issued by the Applegate Ranger District. These can be procured at the Ranger Station, as shown on the map accompanying the previous site (Applegate North), or by writing to the Applegate Ranger District, 6941 Upper Applegate Road, Jacksonville, OR 97530, (541) 899-1812. The fees are discussed within the text describing Applegate North.

For those wanting to use a dredge, it is necessary to procure a valid dredging permit. For dredging in Oregon, write to the Oregon Department of Environmental Quality, 811 SW Sixth Ave., Portland, OR 97204. Ask for the NPDES, 0700-J permit for recreational dredges up to a 4-inch nozzle size. For California areas, contact the California Department of Fish and Game, 601 Locust St., Redding, CA 96001. All sites are open year-round, but dredging in Oregon is limited to July 1 through September 15 unless a waiver is obtained. There are hundreds of valid mining claims in the area, so restrict your prospecting to the specific regions set aside for public use.

To get to Site "A," turn right onto Forest Road 10 from the intersection County Road 859 at the southern tip of Applegate Reservoir and drive four and one-half miles to Sutton Gulch Road. Public prospecting is allowed along 700 linear feet of Carberry Creek. Continue another two and one-half miles, turn left onto Forest Road 1030, and go five and two-tenths miles to a series of flats along Steve Fork Creek. There are roads leading to the creek at both ends of the public area and this is Site "B."

To get to the California locations from County Road 859 and Forest Road 1050, head east one and three-tenths miles, go right three and seven-tenths miles, and park. Prospecting is allowed along the Cook and Green River, and the Middle Fork of the Applegate River labeled Site "C" on the map. About 400 linear feet of Cook and Green Creek and 1600 linear feet along the Middle fork of the Applegate are open to the public.

Site "D" is reached by going eight-tenths of a mile from the turnoff to Site "C" along Forest Road 1050 and turning right one-tenth of a mile to the bridge spanning Elliot Creek at the Hutton Guard Station.

The final gold location is accessed by continuing another two miles along Forest Road 1050 and pulling off alongside Elliot Creek. There are signs designating the public area boundaries.

APPLEGATE SOUTH

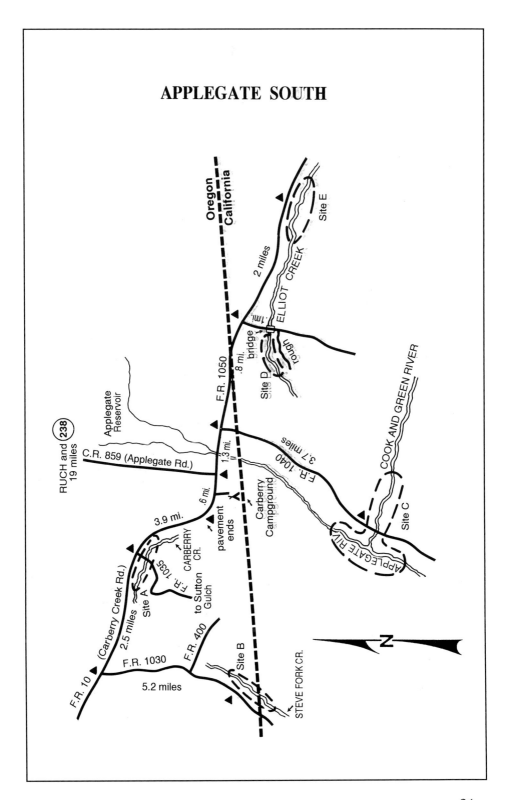

Outstanding but generally small and scarce specimens of petrified wood, agate and jasper can be found on the lower slopes of both Upper and Lower Table Rock, situated about nine miles north of Medford. In addition, more material can be gathered in many of the small streams descending their slopes and on the flatlands below. This entire region is locally known as the Agate Desert. There is still material left, even though so much has been picked up over the years. Due to the proximity of Medford, much of the surrounding land is private, and thereby inaccessible to rockhounds. The Bureau of Land Management, however, maintains two trails which lead through the private regions onto the slopes of both buttes. Note that while in these B.L.M. Preserves no plant or animal life can be disturbed. It is required that you stay on designated trails.

To get to Upper Table Rock, take Exit 33 from Interstate 5 and proceed east nine-tenths of a mile to Table Rock Road. Turn left, continue five and one-tenth miles, and then go right onto Modoc Road. Another one and five-tenths miles farther along, on the left, is the Upper Table Rock Trail parking area. The turnout is a little difficult to spot. Be attentive as you approach the given mileage. From that point, it is necessary to start hiking onto the public lands. Be sure to take water with you. The trail is uphill and the air generally dry. The brightly colored agates and jaspers are easy to spot against the brownish native soil. The petrified wood is more difficult to find, due to its darker coloration. Do not expect the ground to be covered with brilliantly colored material. It takes patience to find much of anything. This is a fairly well-hiked trail. No digging is allowed. Only surface material

may be gathered. To reach the Lower Table Rock Trail, return to Table Rock Road, turn right, and continue two and one-half miles to Wheeler Road, where you should go left. Continue another eight-tenths of a mile and drive left into the trialhead parking area. The material found here is the same as at the previous site and the same restrictions apply. For more information, contact the Bureau of Land Management, 3040 Biddle Road, Medford, Oregon 97501, or call (541) 770-2200.

*Trailhead to
Lower Table Rock*

TABLE ROCK

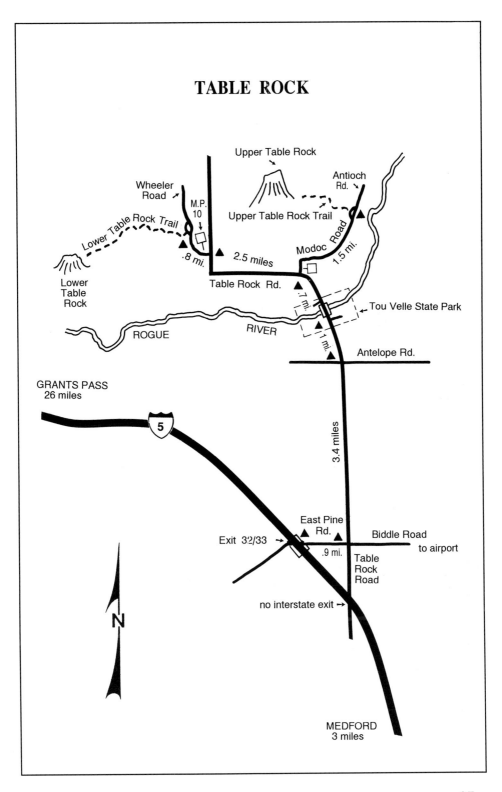

This is one of four places in Oregon where gold bearing streams have been set aside for public recreational prospecting. To get there, go north from Medford about ten miles to Exit 40. Just before entering the town of Gold Hill, turn east onto Highway 234. Be sure to explore Gold Hill, if you have time. It is an interesting place to visit and offers some good insight into the history of the entire area.

From Gold Hill, follow Highway 234, which is the route to Crater Lake, two and three-tenths miles to the Gold Nugget Recreation Area, which is on the banks of the Rogue River. It is within the confines of the Gold Nugget Recreation Area where amateur prospectors can try their luck with pans, sluices or small dredges. No fee is charged, but a valid Oregon dredging permit must be in your possession if you intend to use a dredge. Dredging permits can be obtained from the Oregon Department of Environmental Quality, 811 SW Sixth Avenue, Portland, OR 97204. Ask for the NPDES, 0700-J permit for recreational dredges up to a 4-inch nozzle size. The site is governed by the Medford District, Bureau of Land Management, 3040 Biddle Road, Medford, OR 97504; (541) 770-2200.

Be advised that the Rogue River is a mighty waterway and should be treated with due respect. Do not venture into fast currents or areas you are not equipped to handle. Most recreational gold seekers restrict their efforts to regions immediately adjacent to the shore. Look for places the gold may have been trapped by objects such as boulders or roots, or for spots the current suddenly slows. Both situations provide excellent opportunities for the accumulation of heavy gold.

Do not expect your pan or sluice to be filled with brilliant nuggets. Even though good-sized specimens have been recovered from this part of the Rogue River, most of what amateur prospectors find are very small nuggets and flakes, if anything at all. The area is peaceful, the sound of the running river is soothing, and, even if you don't return home wealthy, you should still have an enjoyable time and have a little gold to show for your efforts.

GOLD NUGGET

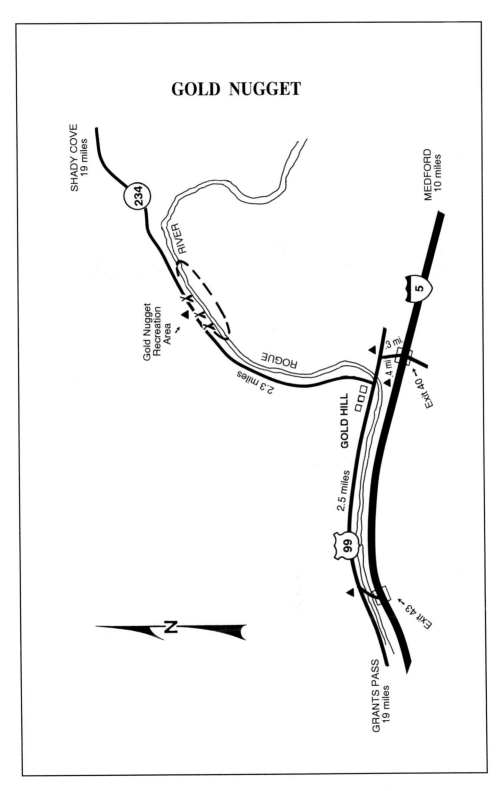

SHADY COVE
19 miles

234

RIVER

Gold Nugget
Recreation
Area

ROGUE

2.3 miles

MEDFORD
10 miles

5

.3 mi.

.4 mi.

Exit 40

GOLD HILL

Exit 43

2.5 miles

99

N

GRANTS PASS
19 miles

Nice, but generally small specimens of petrified wood, jasper, chalcedony and highly desirable moss and dendritic agate can be found throughout the region just north of Medford referred to as the Agate Desert. One fairly productive spot is reached by taking Exit 33 from Interstate 5, heading east on East Pine Road nine-tenths of a mile. Turn left onto Table Rock Road and continue another three and four-tenths miles to Antelope Road, as shown on the accompanying map.

To find the wood and agate, simply park off the pavement anywhere along Antelope Road and stroll through the brush, keeping a sharp eye to the ground. Once you have acquired a few pieces, and get accustomed to the look of the local material, subsequent specimens should be easier to procure. It does not take much effort to find an acceptable quantity of tumbling and cutting size wood and agate. If you are not satisfied with what you find, simply drive a little farther, pull off the pavement, and try again. This spot is especially productive shortly after a rainstorm, if the soil is not too muddy.

Be advised that there is extensive private property along Antelope Road, so be certain not to trespass without first getting permission. There is still so much open area for searching that it really isn't necessary to even consider collecting on private lands. In addition to the Antelope Road locality, it should be noted that virtually every stream or area of erosion in this entire region affords good promise for finding minerals and wood. If you have the time, simply stop at any such location and do some searching. Often, hunting in such random localities will provide larger and better specimens. The banks of the Rogue River, just north of Antelope Road, are also a good place to try your luck. Just be very careful, since the river flows rapidly and could be hazardous if you should slip and fall in.

The banks of the Rouge River

MEDFORD

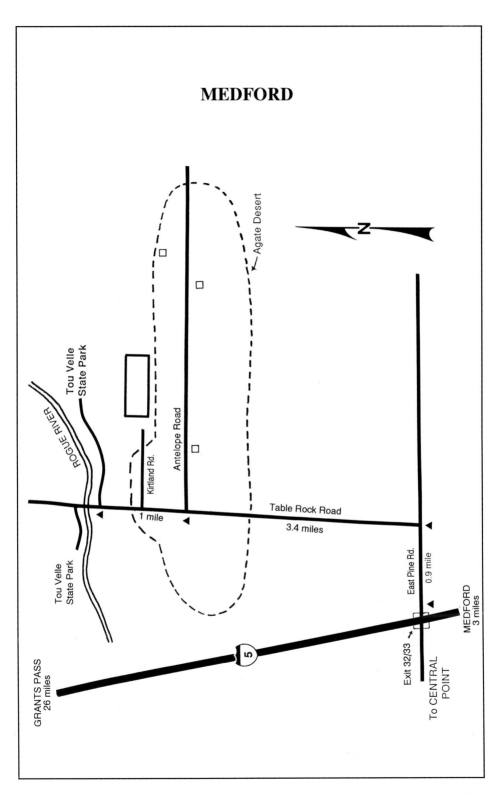

Colorful agate and petrified wood can be found in and around Butte Creek and Antelope Creek, near the town of Eagle Point. This entire region is aptly known as the Agate Desert. The possibility of stumbling upon a nice agate or chunk of petrified wood just about anywhere in the general area is likely. One of the traditionally better-known concentrations is within the territory surrounding the confluence of Butte Creek and Antelope Creek.

To get there from Medford, go north on Highway 62 about eight miles to where Highway 140 intersects. Continue toward Shady Cove three more miles, cross over Butte Creek, and, just beyond is the road to Eagle Point. Instead of turning right toward Eagle Point, however, go left about one-half mile. Look for a good spot to pull off. From wherever you choose to park, just start walking and searching. It is not necessary to get all the way to the river, about one-tenth of a mile to the south, to find specimens. Just look in regions adjacent to the roadway and in open areas, continuing for quite a distance along the road. There is some private land in the area, so be sure to restrict all rockhounding efforts to road shoulders and/or open land.

Another potentially productive area is anywhere between Highway 62 and Eagle Point in and around Butte Creek. Park off the roadway and examine non-private areas. If you want to explore the creeks themselves, the best time of year to conduct such a search is usually during the summer months when water levels are low.

Since most of the agate and wood found in Agate Desert, especially within the Butte Creek/Antelope Creek region, was deposited through the process of erosion, most of the pebbles tend to have abraded surfaces, making them difficult to identify. They will appear dull and uninteresting upon first glance. Look for faint coloration and split any suspect rocks to expose a fresh, unabraded surface in order to evaluate what is actually concealed beneath the surface.

BUTTE CREEK

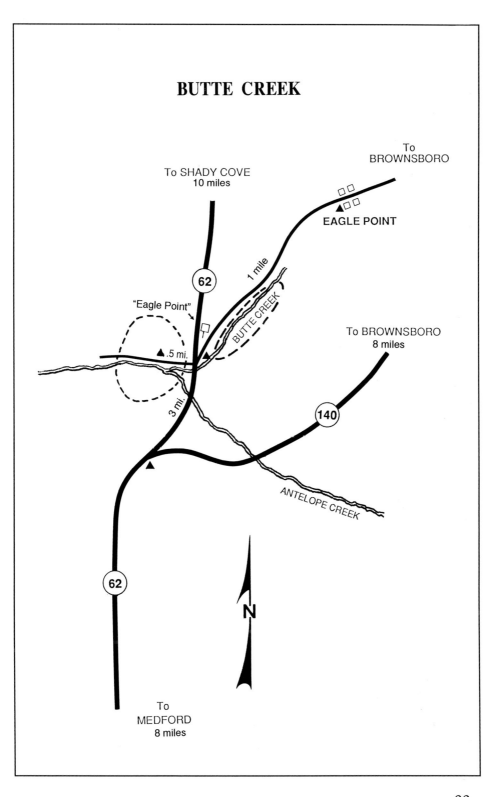

To SHADY COVE
10 miles

To
BROWNSBORO

EAGLE POINT

62

1 mile

"Eagle Point"

BUTTE CREEK

To BROWNSBORO
8 miles

▲ .5 mi.

3 mi.

140

▲

ANTELOPE CREEK

62

N

To
MEDFORD
8 miles

Agate Lake, and the countryside surrounding it, offers rockhounds an opportunity to collect fine specimens of very colorful agate and jasper, petrified wood, chalcedony, and a variety of other minerals. The agate is of primary interest here, since it can be found displaying many different patterns and colors, some of which are quite beautiful.

To get to Agate Lake, take Exit 33 from Interstate 5, go east on East Pine Road two and two-tenths miles, and then turn left onto Highway 62. Go three and four-tenths miles, turn right and continue another three and four-tenths miles to the Agate Lake turnoff sign. Turn right and follow the signs one and three-tenths miles to the lake itself, as illustrated on the map.

It is suggested that you start at Agate Lake. Simply walk around it, keeping an eye out for the agates and other minerals. Nothing is especially large, but good tumbling and cabochon material is relatively easy to find. The banks of the lake are not overly productive, since most of the rocks have become camouflaged with a coating of dried mud. For that reason, it is advisable to branch away from the shore. As you get onto the higher ground, the stones tend to be a little cleaner, thereby making them easier to spot.

There is no particular area of high mineral concentration in the Agate Lake area, so patience and persistence are needed to find worthwhile quantities. It is nice to explore. Before you know it, you will probably be able to gather quite a few nice pieces of agate, jasper, chalcedony and wood.

If you are not satisfied with what can be found, hike through the brush lining nearby Dry Creek. Dry Creek is noted for its fine dendritic and moss agate, but, as was the case before, it will take some effort to find acceptable amounts of material. The entire region surrounding Central Point, Eagle Point, White City and Brownsboro is scattered with agate, jasper and wood. Just about every stream and wash in that territory offers good collecting potential. Be advised that much of the area is privately owned and permission must be granted before you can search these lands. If you see such a spot that looks promising, let the landowner know you are a rockhound

and, with his consent, would like to look around. Most of the local residents are very friendly and will be accommodating, if you have the courtesy to seek permission beforehand.

Parked at Agate Lake

AGATE LAKE

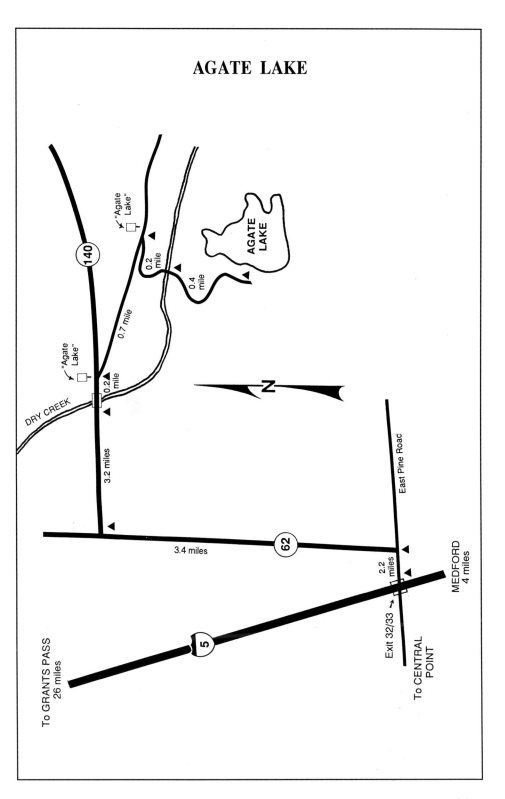

The region east of Ashland provides collectors with fine specimens of agate and geodes, and one of best places to find such minerals is only about seven miles east of Interstate 5. Take Exit 14 and follow Highway 66 east approximately seven and four-tenths miles until dark basalt is spotted in the road cuts, primarily on the left side of the pavement. This outcrop continues at least four miles past milepost 9, and virtually any portion provides potential for finding agate and small crystal-lined geodes. The agate is a secondary mineral here, having filled cracks and seams of the basalt. Such agate-filled fissures are generally easy to spot, since the agate is much lighter in color than the host material. Some of the seams are wider, and offer more potential than others; take a little time to ascertain which might be the best.

It is necessary to use gads and sledge hammers to free the agate within the tough basalt. Be very careful, while working, that nothing is allowed to fall onto the pavement, since such obstacles would create a considerable hazard. In addition, you should be extremely careful when crossing the highway and be certain to park your vehicle in a safe location, well off the pavement. Rapidly moving vehicles are not expecting to encounter pedestrians or stopped vehicles on this winding stretch of road. It is recommended, after determining where the best agate seams are located, to move onto upper basalt regions for easier and less hazardous working conditions.

Another good place to find quality agate is at nearby Emigrant Lake. You should also be able to find lots of agate pebbles, especially if the water is low. Walk along the shore keeping an eye out for the nice cutting material. Note that fossils can be found in many of the road cuts near Ashland. It might be worth your time, if one looks promising, to stop and investigate. Some of the Ashland fossils are interesting and make great display pieces.

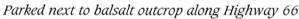

Parked next to balsalt outcrop along Highway 66

ASHLAND

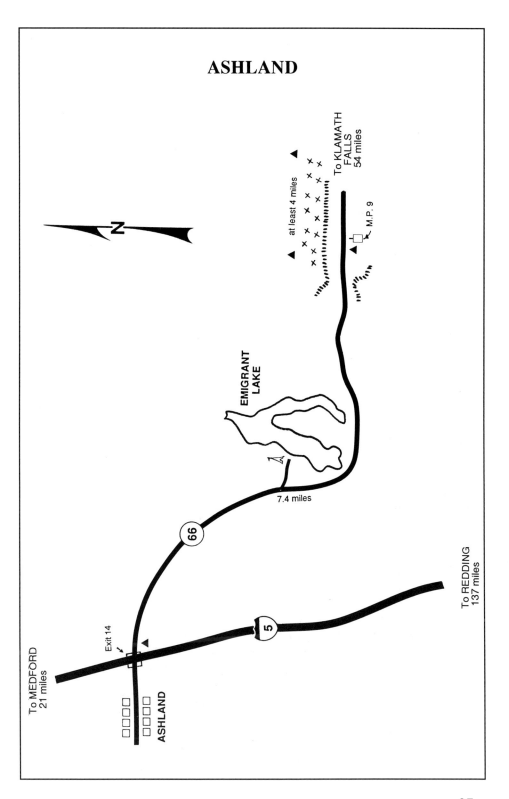

To MEDFORD
21 miles

ASHLAND

Exit 14

66

5

To REDDING
137 miles

7.4 miles

EMIGRANT
LAKE

at least 4 miles

To KLAMATH
FALLS
54 miles

M.P. 9

N

Serpentine, rhodonite, and jade lead the list of what can be found in and around many of the streams and rivers near Happy Camp, California, situated just south of the Oregon border. In addition, rockhounds can also gather nice nodules of bowenite, as well as idocrase crystals, garnet and pyrite. Probably the best collecting is at Site "A." At one time this was a private claim. At time of publication, the status of the claim was unclear, but it appeared still available to amateur rockhounding. It might be wise, however, to attempt to determine the collecting status in town before heading in.

To get there, park at the mileage depicted on the map and walk down to the river's edge. The jade and serpentine are fairly easy to spot, due to their green color. Locating rhodonite is not as easy, since it is usually covered with an unappealing black crust. Due to the "camouflage," be sure to split any suspect black stones in hopes of exposing beautiful pink interiors. Walk a distance, in either direction, alongside the stream. Carefully examine stones in the creek, as well as on its banks. If you are unsatisfied with what can be obtained from the surface, digging may expose additional specimens. If you wade in the creek, be very careful, since many of the rocks are coated with a slick moss which may cause you to lose your footing.

Site "B," on the west branch of Indian Creek, offers similar material in smaller amounts. In fact, just about any of the creeks in the region have potential. Just be sure not to trespass onto private property without first getting permission.

Serpentine and occasional pieces of jade can be found in the abandoned quarry designated as Site "C." As is the case with any mine, be certain to collect in safe locations, be on the lookout for hidden pits, and, under no circumstances, enter a shaft.

The minerals are fairly easy to obtain by digging through the rubble. The telltale green color of the serpentine and jade make it easy to spot. Pieces range in size from tiny chips and pebbles to large boulders and the quality also has a considerably wide range. Remember that the collecting status of old mines changes from time to time, so if there are any indications the quarry has been reactivated, be sure to inquire before digging.

Site "D" offers an additional opportunity to gather more jade and serpentine. The material here tends to be less fractured than that from Site "C," thereby being slightly more desirable for cutting and polishing. The search is more challenging here, though, since the ground is covered with thick brush and trees. Pull safely off the road and carefully climb on the hillsides to find the minerals.

HAPPY CAMP

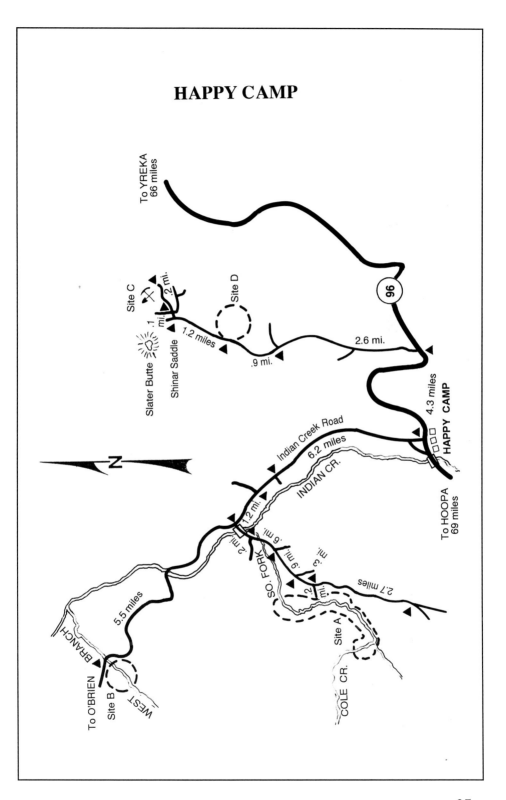

To YREKA
66 miles

96

Site C

.2 mi.

Site D

Slater Butte

.1 mi.

Shinar Saddle

1.2 miles

.9 mi.

2.6 mi.

4.3 miles

HAPPY CAMP

Indian Creek Road

6.2 miles

INDIAN CR.

N

1.2 mi.

.2 mi.

.6 mi.

.3 mi.

SO. FORK

.9 mi.

.2 mi.

2.7 miles

To HOOPA
69 miles

Site A

COLE CR.

5.5 miles

WEST BRANCH

To O'BRIEN

Site B

95

Hammers

Probably the one piece of equipment most identified with rockhounding and prospecting is the hand-held rock pick. Generally, one side of the head is blunt and flat, while the opposite is either pointed or chisel shaped. If there is only one tool you can take on a field trip, this surely would be the most useful for most situations. The flattened end is handy for cracking small rocks and driving chisels or gads into seams or cracks. The pointed or flattened end is good for light digging or for prying open cracks.

A sledge hammer is extremely helpful if you need to break up sizable pieces of rock or are trying to extract gems still encased in seams or cavities. A sledge hammer also supplies more power for pounding chisels or gads into hard rock, or for breaking off samples from an outcrop. Sledge hammers come in a variety of weights and are available with short or long handles.

Rock Chisels, Gads, and Star Drills

A rock chisel is a hand tool, with a sharpened flat end, used to trim specimens, chip off samples, or to split rocks and seams. A gad is a similar hand tool, but, instead of having a flat end, it is pointed. Gads are primarily used to break up rock or are inserted in cracks or seams to split them open.

Gads are more useful to rockhounds, since their pointed and tapered ends tend to get farther inside cracks and crevices than chisels. A star drill looks much like a gad, but it is thinner and primarily used to make holes in rock within which a gad can be inserted to do its job.

Gads, chisels, and star drills can be purchased in a variety of widths, lengths and weights. As is the case with hammers, be certain to obtain only those designed for use on rock.

Trowel

A trowel is a small hand-held digging tool which is very helpful when exploring mine dumps, washes, or regions where light digging of soft surface soil is required.

Pry Bar

Pry bars often come in handy when working hard rock seams or cavities. Furthermore, they can be used to break up tough soil and move large boulders. Pry bars afford better leverage than smaller hand tools and are much stronger, thereby being less likely to bend or break.

Pick and Shovel

Picks and shovels are needed when you must dig to locate minerals. At many sites, the surface material has all been taken, but, not too far below, there are still lots of excellent specimens. Getting to those otherwise hidden stones is made possible by using a pick and shovel.

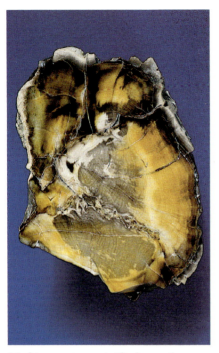

Jasper from the Ashwood area

Stinkingwater petrified wood

Succor Creek picture jasper

Miscellaneous Oregon obsidian

Polished McDermitt rhyolite

Agate from Ashwood area

*Tumble polished petrified wood
from McDermitt*

Thundereggs from Richardson's Ranch

Polka-Dot agate from Ashwood

"Worm Hole Rock"
from Bates

Biggs picture rock and McDermitt
wonderstone

Blue and white jasper from Ashwood Area

Green "Oregon Jade" jasper and a slab of jade

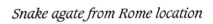

Snake agate from Rome location

Maury Mountain red and green jasper

*Beach agates and jaspers
(polished)*

Agate from Ashwood area

Agate from Ashwood area

Holly Blue agate (Calapooia River)

Jasper from Richardson's Ranch

Sunstone from Hart Mountain

Fossil bearing rock from near Juntura

Graveyard Point agate

Oregon carnelian agate

A round ended shovel is the best for digging, while the most efficient pick is a mattock. One side of a mattock's digging end is pointed and the opposite side is flat and chisel-like. A mattock pick is capable of doing all kinds of digging, from precise trenching to large scale dirt moving. The pointed end offers excellent penetration, especially if working in hard soil, and, once the soil is loosened, the chisel end is great for removing dirt quickly.

Safety Goggles

Safety goggles are a must when doing any hammering onto hard rock. Rock fragments or splintered metal from your hammer can fly off at the speed of a bullet when struck, thereby creating a potentially hazardous situation.

Hat and Proper Clothing

Taking clothing appropriate to the location(s) you will be visiting is essential if you want the trip to be an enjoyable experience. Be prepared for just about anything. Rain, mud, extremely hot weather, extremely cold weather, and even insects. Do some research on the region you plan to visit. Will you be in the barren and desolate desert or rugged mountains? Should you expect snow or rain, or will it be scorching hot?

Footwear is also of prime importance. Wear shoes appropriate to the terrain you will be exploring. If going to wet areas, waterproof shoes would be nice, as would an extra dry pair. If in hot and arid regions, shoes that "breathe" should be considered.

Gloves

If you plan to do anything except pick up specimens from the surface, gloves are recommended. Using a rock pick or sledge hammer for a few hours, or digging with pick and shovel, can cause painful blisters, cuts, and abrasions on one's hands. The associated tenderness and pain can quickly take the joy out of a collecting expedition. A good pair of gloves can make such handicaps less likely.

Collecting Bag or Backpack

When you visit a collecting site, it will probably be necessary to do some walking from where you park, and it is surprising how far you might stray. There is a limit to how much a person can carry in their pockets and hands, however, and that limit seems to always be reached just before coming upon the most beautiful specimen of your hike. A sturdy bag or backpack made from canvas or rip-stop nylon comes in quite handy in situations like this.

From *The Rockhound's Handbook* by James R. Mitchell

This location is actually in California, just south of the Oregon border, and boasts jasper, rhodonite, carnelian, agate and petrified wood. Take Exit 788 from Interstate 5 and head east on Copco Road twelve and seven-tenths miles to Jenny Creek.

Material can be found all along the banks of Jenny Creek continuing north from near where it passes the Wilkes Expedition Memorial, at the Iron Gate Reservoir and all the way into Oregon. Search on both sides of the road paralleling the creek, as well as in the creek itself. Pay particularly close attention to any stone spotted in the soft soil of the banks or in other areas of erosion. Be sure to also inspect the roadbeds and berms, especially if freshly graded.

It is usually easy to spot the gemstones, since their bright colors tend to stand out vividly against the darker native soil. The only exception is the rhodonite, which may be encrusted with a black layer of oxidation. Use a rock pick to split any such stones in hopes of exposing a prize pink interior.

None of the minerals is overly plentiful at any particular place, but concentrations vary from spot to spot. The colorful jasper seems to be the most frequently encountered, and is of high quality, occurring in a variety of often brilliant colors, including red, yellow, rust and orange. The agate is generally found in darker shades, usually containing interesting inclusions. Brown and tan petrified wood can also be picked up in the environs of Jenny Creek, but it is not plentiful.

Jenny Creek

JENNY CREEK

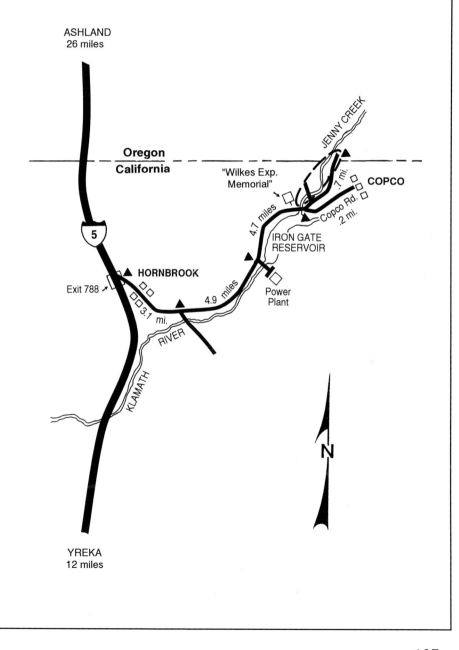

ASHLAND
26 miles

Oregon
California

"Wilkes Exp.
Memorial"

JENNY CREEK

COPCO

Copco Rd.
.2 mi.

.7 mi.

4.7 miles

5

IRON GATE
RESERVOIR

HORNBROOK

Exit 788

3.1 mi.

4.9 miles

Power
Plant

RIVER

KLAMATH

N

YREKA
12 miles

This location is in California, a short distance south of the Oregon border, and it is centered in a region known throughout the country for its top grade obsidian. Go south from Lakeview (Oregon) about twenty-nine miles on Highway 395 to the paved turnoff leading to the east, as illustrated on the accompanying map. This is Sugar Hill Pit Road. Continue northeast four and four-tenths miles to the turnoff to Site "A." At Site "A" one can pick up many fine obsidian specimens over a very large area. Simply park within the general boundaries shown on the accompanying map and hike in any direction. The ground is literally covered with volcanic glass.

Site "A" extends on both sides of the road, especially on the hill to the south. This particular spot is noted for the fine sheen obsidian that can be found here. Material is scattered all over and very little effort is needed to find it. The sizes at both Sites "A" and "B" tend to be small, but a few boulders can also be found amongst the pine needles.

All the way from Site "A" to Site "B," one can find tons of beautiful obsidian, but try not to be tempted to stop. The material at Site "B" is worth the abstinence along the way. At one time this was a private gem obsidian claim, but now seems to be abandoned. If that is not the case when you visit, previous owners have allowed collectors to dig here, for a small fee. At Site "B," numerous pits will be seen where others have dug. This site offers about the best variety of obsidian types available. The list of what can be

found is extensive, and highlighted by golden, green, blue and silver sheen obsidian, as well as rainbow, black and mahogany varieties. Plenty of material can be picked up from the surface, and, if you do some digging, nearly every boulder will be worth inspecting. The pick and shovel work is relatively easy since the soil is soft but be sure to wear goggles and gloves, since the sharp splinters can be sent flying through the air if you strike a chunk of the volcanic glass.

Collecting at Site "B"

LASSEN CREEK

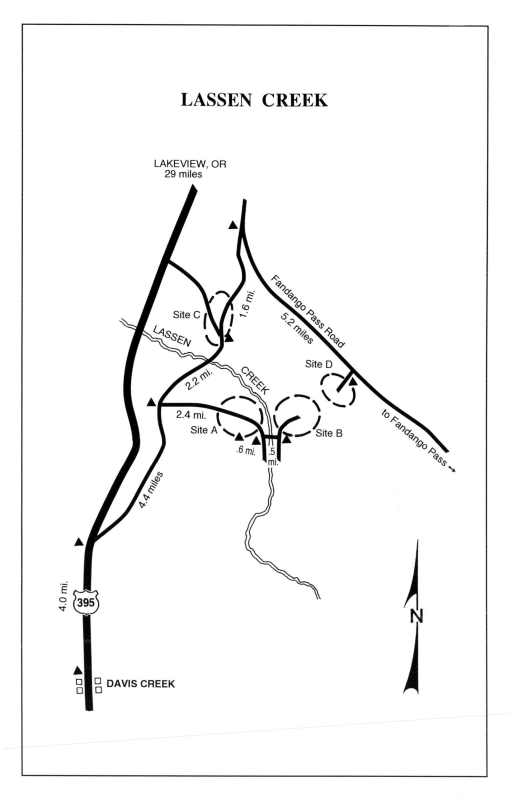

LAKEVIEW, OR
29 miles

Fandango Pass Road
5.2 miles

to Fandango Pass →

Site C

1.6 mi.

LASSEN

CREEK

Site D

2.2 mi.

2.4 mi.

Site A

Site B

.6 mi.

.5 mi.

4.4 miles

4.0 mi.

395

N

DAVIS CREEK

This location is situated just south of the Oregon border in California. This provides collectors with a chance to obtain exceptional specimens of obsidian needles, as well as a seemingly unlimited quantity of more common obsidian varieties. Always keep in mind that obsidian is glass and shatters easily. For that reason, rockhounds are reminded to wear gloves and goggles if planning to do any splitting of specimens.

To get to the first stop, Site "A," turn off Highway 395 in Davis Creek and head east to the cemetery which is about eight-tenths of a mile away. At that point there is a three-way fork, bear onto the center choice. Just past that fork is the center of Site "A."

This spot is extensive, consisting of acres of obsidian covered flatlands. Most of what can be found at Site "A" is black, but nice brown material is also available. The quality is generally good, but sizes tend to be somewhat small. The best way to collect here is to park and roam through the flatlands, picking up anything that looks promising.

At Site "B," it is necessary to hike up a steep trail to the main area where rainbow obsidian can be acquired. In order to find the highly prized rainbow material, it is usually necessary to do some digging. The soil is soft, though, making that chore fairly easy. To determine if you have unearthed any rainbow pieces, chip off a portion and wet the surface. When held in the sun, the colors of the spectrum should be visible. This spot also provides lots of black, brown and flow material. Site "C" is similar to Site "A," but the terrain is more mountainous and tree covered. Sizes tend to be a little larger. There seems to be a greater percentage of gem material here. Site "C" starts at the intersection shown on the map and continues for quite a distance eastward, both north and south of the road. Site "D" is well-known throughout the West for its fascinating obsidian needles. In fact, the central knoll is called Obsidian Needle Hill. The glassy needles cover the western slopes and it takes very little effort to gather hundreds of them. In addition to the unusual needles, one can find black, brown and double flow specimens, some display attractive bands and swirls. Most of what can be gathered at Site "D" is gem quality and the quantity is seemingly unlimited.

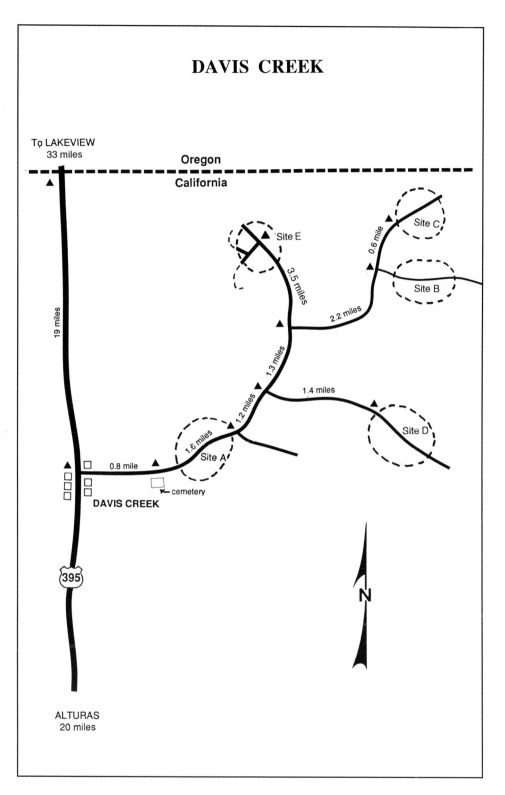

DAVIS CREEK

To LAKEVIEW
33 miles

Oregon

California

19 miles

Site E

3.5 miles

0.6 mile

Site C

Site B

2.2 miles

1.3 miles

1.4 miles

1.2 miles

Site D

1.6 miles

Site A

0.8 mile

cemetery

DAVIS CREEK

395

N

ALTURAS
20 miles

The region bounded by Drews Reservoir, Dog Lake and Dry Creek is well known among Oregon rockhounds for its good quality opalized wood, agate, jasper and jasp-agate. Due to that long-standing popularity, material is somewhat scarce, and concentrations random. Just about anywhere within the area offers rockhounding promise.

To get to Site "A," which is primarily known for its opalized wood, take Highway 140 about eight miles west from Lakeview and then turn south. Drive four more miles, turn right, go another three miles to the National Forest boundary, and then continue straight ahead on Forest Road 4017 about three and one-half additional miles to where a little road leads off to the right, just west of Drews Reservoir. The opalized wood tends to be scattered throughout the terrain as illustrated on the map and it takes some patience to find. You can either search for specimens on the surface or dig for them. It is often helpful to rake away the ground cover to expose fresh soil and rock, since much is hidden. Look for where previous rockhounds have been excavating for ideas as to where you should start and don't be afraid to do some hiking into the forest.

Site "B" encompasses a region alongside the road to Dry Creek, as shown on the map. For quite a distance along the road, starting just inside the National Forest boundary, an abundance of nice agate, jasper and jasp-agate can be picked up. Scattered concentrations will be found almost all the way to Dry Creek itself, which is actually in California, about fifteen miles from where you cross into the National Forest. At Dry Creek Ridge, thundereggs can be obtained. Determining exactly where to dig takes some luck and persistence. Look for signs of broken thundereggs and/or pits left by previous collectors for clues as to where you should start.

DOG LAKE

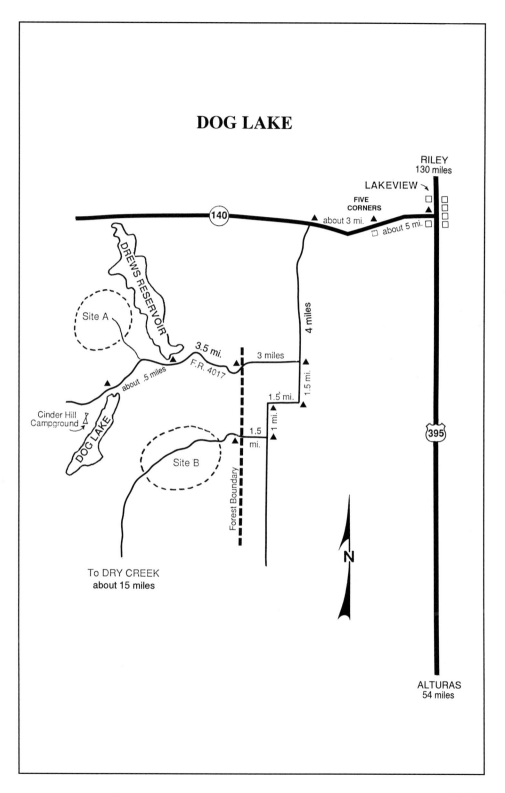

RILEY
130 miles

LAKEVIEW

FIVE
CORNERS

about 3 mi.

about 5 mi.

140

DREWS RESERVOIR

Site A

3.5 mi.

3 miles

4 miles

F.R. 4017

about 5 miles

1.5 mi.

Cinder Hill
Campground

1.5 mi.

DOG LAKE

1 mi.

1.5
mi.

Site B

Forest Boundary

N

To DRY CREEK
about 15 miles

395

ALTURAS
54 miles

113

This petrified wood location is one of many rockhounding sites protected for hobbyists by a legal claim maintained by the Prineville - Crook County Chamber of Commerce. It is a great spot for obtaining petrified wood, since most specimens have retained their original grain and surface structures. Pieces containing knots and little stems are common here, and the digging is relatively easy. Up-to-date information about this and other nearby sites is available at the Prineville - Crook County Chamber of Commerce, located at 390 N. Fairview Street, in Prineville (541) 447-6304.

As you travel to the collecting area, you will pass through a gate and it is mandatory to close it after passing through. The site itself is not tough to find, since the ground is inundated with pits. In fact, it is imperative that you drive carefully when approaching, in order to prevent driving into any of them.

There are small petrified wood chips scattered all over the surrounding terrain, especially near and in the pits. The largest and best-preserved specimens are obtained by doing some pick and shovel work. It is generally necessary to dig a few feet below the surface to hit anything worthwhile, but the soil is relatively soft. The problem is knowing where to dig in the first place. Sometimes you can shovel for hours and not hit anything, while, at other times, you might strike a buried stump with the first swing of your pick. This is one of those locations where some patience and hard work are required to find the best it has to offer. A good policy is to start excavating where it appears previous collectors have had success, rather that to try to find your own new spot. Look for signs of wood chips and chunks around pits for indications of potential. Some beautiful petrified logs have been found here, but they are quite heavy and generally impossible for amateurs to dig out and remove. Most rockhounds restrict their collecting to more

manageable limb sections and pieces. Be sure to also read the information in the Introduction about government-set limits on how much petrified wood any collector can procure. Be sure to take extra food, water and digging equipment, since this is a somewhat remote place and supplies are not available for quite a few dusty miles.

Pit left by previous rockhounds

BEAR CREEK

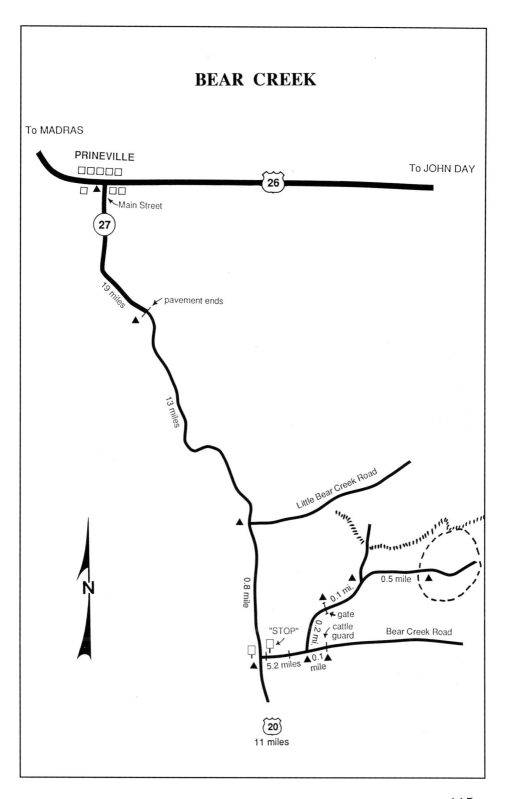

To MADRAS

PRINEVILLE

To JOHN DAY

26

Main Street

27

19 miles

pavement ends

13 miles

Little Bear Creek Road

N

0.8 mile

0.5 mile

0.1 mi.

gate

"STOP"

0.2 mi.

cattle
guard

Bear Creek Road

5.2 miles

0.1
mile

20

11 miles

Outstanding agatized limb casts can be found about fifty miles southeast of Prineville. These highly prized mineralogical oddities were formed countless years ago when the region was covered by a lake. When climates changed, the lake dried up, the surrounding trees died, and their roots and branches subsequently became embedded in the mud. The mud dried and the trees slowly began disintegrating. In time, all that was left were perfect hollow molds of where the roots and branches once were. In ensuing years, these voids were slowly filled with chalcedony, sometimes containing impurities which give the casts their color and interesting internal inclusions. The casts are occasionally clear, but frequently occur in shades of pink, blue, white and green.

Six different sites are depicted, and if you have the time, it would be worth the effort to explore all of them. Colors and inclusions vary from spot to spot. The sites are protected for amateur rockhound use by the Prineville - Crook County Chamber of Commerce and there is no charge to collect. For safety reasons, however, they are closed during hunting season.

The limb casts are found at an average depth of approximately eighteen inches, making it necessary to dig for them. Occasionally, limb casts are discovered on or near the surface, especially near areas of erosion. Pay particularly close attention to the banks overlooking washes and streams, as well as in the waterways themselves.

Site "A" boasts primarily green limb casts, while those from Site "B" tend to be blue and green. Most of the dendritic material is found at Sites "C" and "D," while Site "F" offers predominantly pink hues. Site "E," the least prolific of all the spots, contains randomly colored specimens scattered widely within the gravel surrounding the landing strip. This is a fun place to explore, and the digging isn't too hard. Look for pits and excavations left by previous rockhounds for ideas as to where to start.

Site "D"

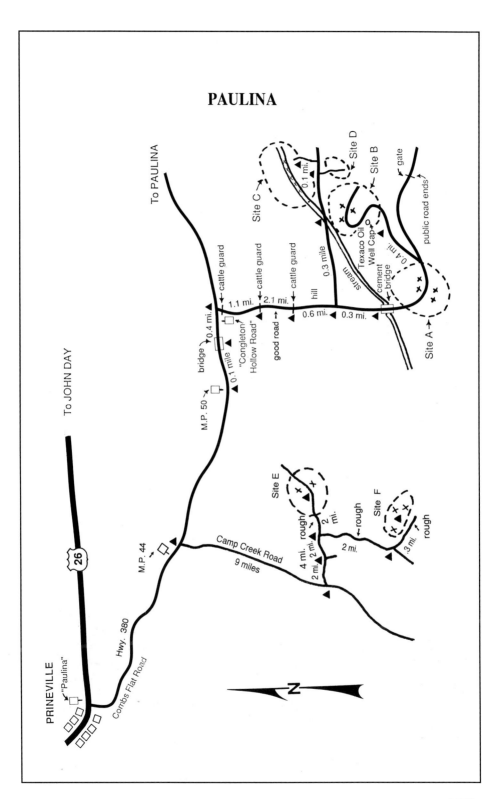

PAULINA

117

Very colorful petrified wood can be found near Hampton Butte, as shown on the accompanying map. Most tends to be jasperized and the colors include brown, black, red, orange, white, and a prized bright green. Some of the green material includes red areas, looking something like bloodstone in the shape of twigs and branches. In addition, colorful agatized wood can also be found here, as can occasional chunks of chalcedony, banded agate and a beautiful multicolored agate.

To get to the center of this interesting and productive site, continue east a short distance from milepost 52, on Highway 20, to Van Lake Road. Turn north, continue ten and four-tenths miles to G.I. Ranch Road, and go right about two more miles. As you approach the given mileage, there are many tracks leading north off G. I. Ranch Road and it does not make any difference which one(s) you choose. Drive only a short distance, get out of you vehicle and do a little walking.

It will not take long before you start finding pieces of the colorful wood, much of which accurately displays the original wood structure. It is not uncommon to procure specimens with knots, branches and even worm holes, all helping to make this one of Oregon's favorite petrified wood localities. It is a good idea to have a small container filled with water nearby, in which you can rinse what you find to ascertain the quality and color.

Larger pieces of the brightly colored wood make outstanding display pieces. Such sizable material usually requires some digging to obtain. For that reason, don't forget to take a pick and shovel. The soil is somewhat soft, making the excavation work relatively easy, and the potential rewards more than compensate for that extra effort. When driving on any of the numerous ruts leading off the G. I. Ranch Road, look for places where others have dug before. This is an indication of where you should start. Be certain, however, if you do any pick and shovel work, that you REFILL ALL HOLES BEFORE LEAVING, since cattle graze here and could become seriously injured by stepping into one.

The primary collecting area is widespread and should provide you with more than enough of the highly regarded Hampton Butte wood. If have some extra time, it might be productive to explore nearby regions, outside the zone shown on the map. Such localities are not as heavily collected and thereby might afford you the chance of stumbling upon something more unusual or sizable. This is a nice place to spend some time and such exploration might not only be fun, but also profitable.

HAMPTON BUTTE

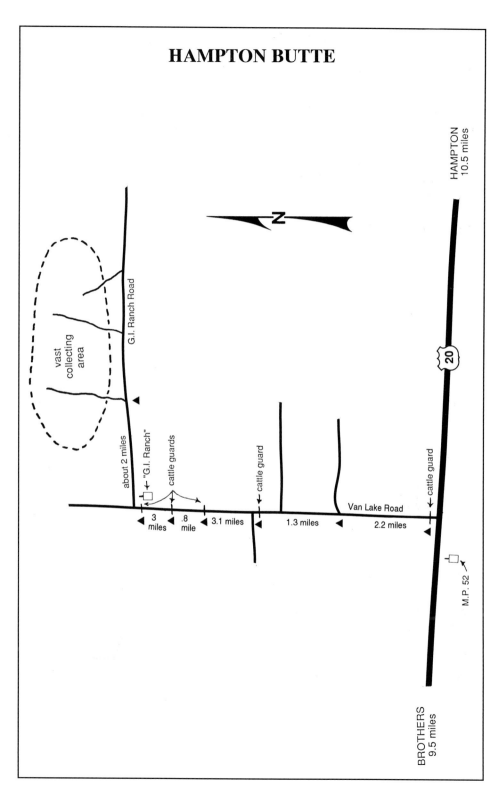

N

HAMPTON
10.5 miles

G.I. Ranch Road

vast
collecting
area

about 2 miles

→ "G.I. Ranch"

cattle guards

← cattle guard

← cattle guard

Van Lake Road

← cattle guard

3
miles

.8
mile

3.1 miles

1.3 miles

2.2 miles

20

M.P. 52

BROTHERS
9.5 miles

This is indisputably Oregon's premier obsidian site. There are many other locations that offer gem quality volcanic glass, but none can match the variety and consistent quality available here. This is virtually a supermarket for obsidian. Within a very tight radius, one can obtain gold sheen, silver sheen, mahogany, red, flame, lace, jet black, double flow, brown, snowflake and highly prized rainbow material. This site is so prolific that gem grade specimens can even be found along the road leading in from the highway.

Of all the various digging sites at Glass Butte, the rainbow excavations are probably the most highly regarded. As you might expect, that site is also the most remote and difficult to get to. Follow the well-traveled dirt tracks, as illustrated on the map, and you will find yourself near pits left by previous rockhounds. It is there you should start to work, hoping to unearth some chunks of that elusive and beautiful volcanic glass.

The two sheen sites, pinpointed on the map, are also well worth stopping at. Obviously, all material found there will not show an iridescent, colorful internal glow, but quite a lot does. Once again, look for the holes left by previous collectors for indications as to where work should be started.

Mahogany Hill is interesting, being a miniature mountain of solid, cutting quality, mahogany obsidian. There is so much available, and the quality is so high, that it almost becomes overwhelming trying to sort out the best.

Showing only six specific collecting sites on the map in no way should imply that those are the only places you should inspect. It is not out of the question to stumble upon something of value. While driving on any of the ruts that crisscross through the Glass Butte area, keep an eye out for places where previous rockhounds have been digging. Those pits often indicate something special was found there, and it might be worth making a stop to investigate.

An important word of caution is essential here. Be certain you do not attack an obsidian deposit without wearing gloves and eye protection. Sharp glass splinters and chips fly through the air when struck with a hammer, and severe eye damage could be caused by just one of them.

GLASS BUTTE

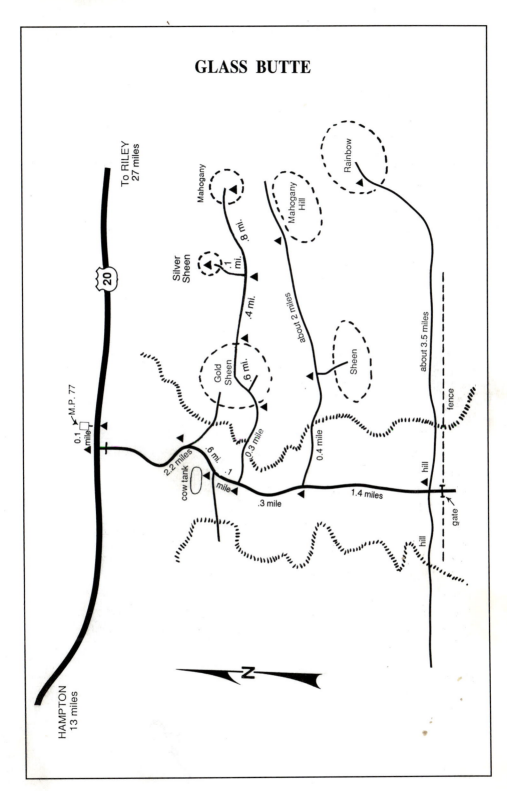

Good quality opalite, interesting cinnabar and an abundance of gem obsidian can all be found scattered throughout the region shown on the map. The roads were originally constructed to serve the cinnabar mines which can be seen on the hills south of Highway 20. Most of these mines are now abandoned, and their dumps offer interesting mineral specimens.

To get there continue seven-tenths of mile east from milepost 81, on Highway 20, and turn right. A stop sign can be seen at this intersection, making the turnoff easy to spot. Just after leaving the highway you will see opalite and obsidian scattered all over the ground. The opalite tends to occur in shades of yellow, cream, white and orange. Most is somewhat fractured, but it does not take much effort to locate good solid pieces. The best opalite is found on the mine dumps. It is suggested you head there first. The final stretch of road leading up to the dumps is not bad, but a rugged vehicle is advisable. In the flatlands, as you approach the mines, the obsidian tends to be jet black. Variegated, double flow and silver sheen material are not uncommon. Prize red, gold and rainbow sheen obsidian, as well as nice red cinnabar specimens can be found nearer the mines. Plenty of time should be allocated to find some examples of each.

Be careful when exploring the dump areas, since there are a few open pits. In addition to inspecting the dumps themselves, be sure to also scour the surrounding terrain as best you can.

While in the area, more gem obsidian can be found about eight miles south of Riley, on Highway 395. If you do visit this location, be sure to park your vehicle well off the pavement while collecting.

Remnants of the old cinnabar mining area

RILEY

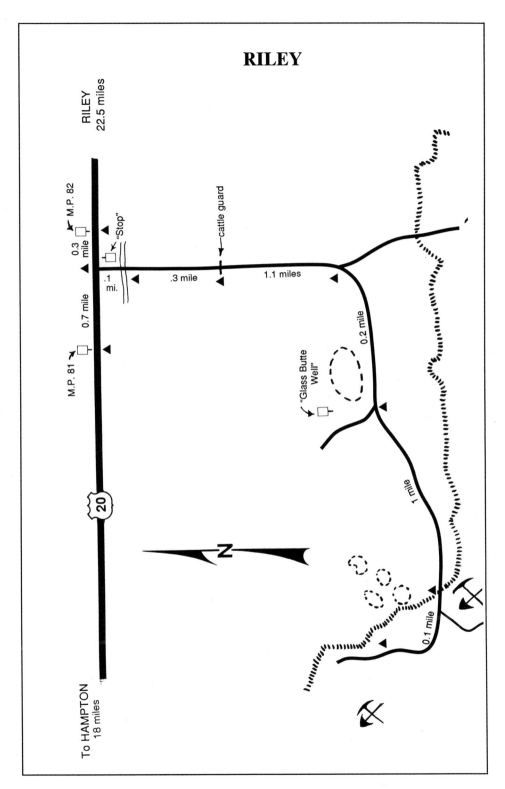

RILEY
22.5 miles

M.P. 82

"Stop"

0.3 mile

.1 mi.

0.7 mile

M.P. 81

cattle guard

.3 mile

1.1 miles

0.2 mile

"Glass Butte Well"

1 mile

0.1 mile

N

20

To HAMPTON
18 miles

The mountains surrounding Hines and Burns are literally made of glass. An abundance of gem obsidian can be found in that region, and only a few of the countless deposits are illustrated on the accompanying map. More information about Burns and other Harney County sites can be obtained at the Highland Rock and Gift Shop at 1316 Hines Blvd. in Burns.

To get to the first of the four specific spots discussed here, proceed northwest on Forest Road 47 from where it intersects Highway 20, just south of town, as illustrated on the accompanying map. Site "A" was, at one time, the location of a large radar tower. The tower is now gone, but the ground is covered with good grade obsidian for quite a distance along the road shown on the map. Jet black material predominates here, but banded and sheen obsidian can also be picked up, as can small Apache tears.

Site "B" and Site "C" both boast large amounts of banded and sheen obsidian. The material is scattered all over the ground, within the boundaries illustrated on the map. It is so thick in places, that the soil appears to be black. Digging isn't necessary since so much is available on the surface. Huge chunks of medium to low grade obsidian can be obtained at the quarry near Site "C," but nothing really worthwhile. Site "D" is extensive, and, as was the case with Sites "A," "B" and "C," gem grade obsidian can be found scattered over the terrain. The collecting starts about three-tenths of a mile from the pavement and continues on both sides of the road, for at least another eight miles. At the six-mile mark, pass through a gate. Just past that gate are some ruts leading to the right. Follow them a short distance where unusual, small chunks of bright red obsidian can be found. At the seven and one-half-mile mark, sheen and peacock obsidian can be removed from the road cuts. Site "D" offers plenty of variety. The road isn't too bad, but rugged vehicles are advisable. Be sure to close all gates in Site "D."

Parked at a quarry across from Site "C"

HINES

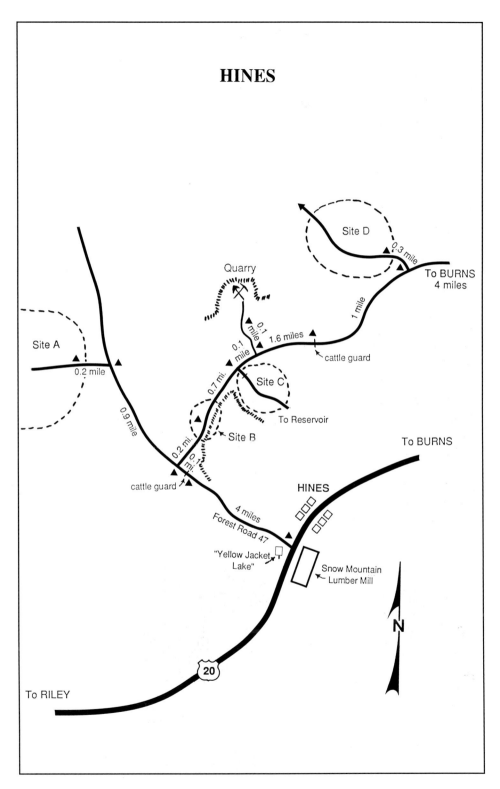

Site D

0.3 mile

To BURNS
4 miles

Quarry

1 mile

0.1 mile

0.1 mile

1.6 miles

cattle guard

Site A

0.2 mile

Site C

0.7 mi.

To Reservoir

0.9 mile

0.2 mi.

Site B

0.1 mi.

cattle guard

To BURNS

HINES

4 miles

Forest Road 47

"Yellow Jacket Lake"

Snow Mountain
Lumber Mill

N

20

To RILEY

This would be an interesting place to visit, even if it wasn't such a great collecting location. Both sites offer top quality cutting materials, including very colorful agate, jasper and petrified wood. Go south on Highway 205 about twenty-four miles from where it intersects Highway 78 near Burns. You will pass through the Malheur National Wildlife Refuge where you can view countless native birds and other wildlife.

Just before reaching milepost 24, turn right and continue one and one-half miles to where a number of gravel mounds and a large pit will be seen. Those landmarks make up Site "A." The gravel mounds contain a very high percentage of colorful agate, jasper and petrified wood. If you want abundant top grade, ready to tumble material, plan to spend some time here. There are other pits and mounds in the region, and all offer equal potential. Note that the gravel on the road leading from Site "A" to Site "B" is also filled with the petrified wood, agate and jasper pebbles, and it might be worth your time to make a few stops to see what can be found.

The tracks leading up the mesa to Site "B" are very steep and only rugged vehicles should attempt going there. Four-wheel drive will probably be necessary if the road is wet. Simply park and walk the short distance if you have any doubts about whether your vehicle can make it. You might even be rewarded on the way up with some nice chunks of agate and jasper.

The mineral of primary interest at Site "B" is a fascinating oolitic agate. One can find many other agate varieties, as well as some nice petrified wood. The wood is believed to be birch, and some is even opalized. Such pieces often can be used to make showy cabochons or simply displayed as is. The Stinkingwater Rock Club holds a claim at Site "B," but rockhounds are usually welcome. If there is any indication that status has changed, be sure to respect the rights of the claim holders.

View of Site "B" from down below

MALHEUR LAKE

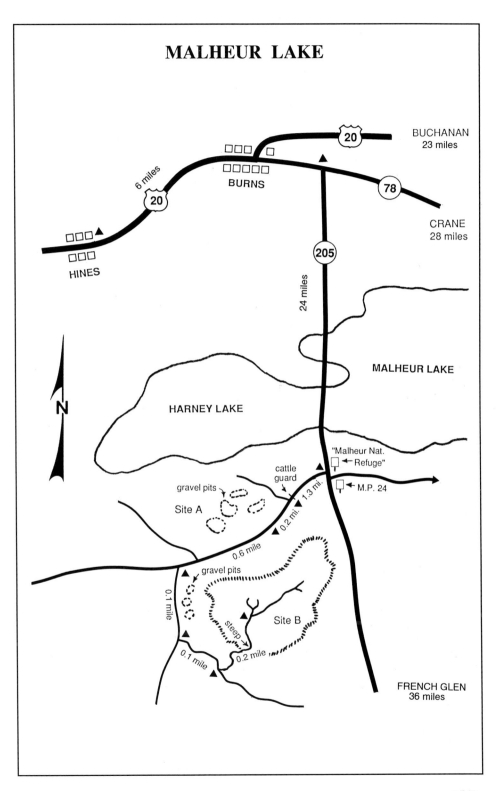

BUCHANAN
23 miles

20

BURNS

6 miles

20

78

CRANE
28 miles

HINES

205

24 miles

MALHEUR LAKE

N

HARNEY LAKE

"Malheur Nat.
Refuge" ←

cattle
guard ↓

← M.P. 24

gravel pits →

Site A

0.2 mi. 1.3 mi.

0.6 mile

gravel pits

0.1 mile

steep ↓

Site B

0.1 mile

0.2 mile

FRENCH GLEN
36 miles

This is not a collecting site, but is an area of fascinating geological significance. The region referred to as Diamond Craters encompasses an isolated volcanic field at the southern edge of Harney Basin and exhibits many unusual features that exist nowhere else in Oregon. Diamond Craters comprises an area over six miles in diameter with a history of active volcanism dating back at least one million years, with the most recent eruptions taking place only a few hundred years ago.

Three especially unique features distinguish Diamond Craters from other such regions. First, is the large and nearly perfect Graben Dome which exhibits little trace of weathering or erosion to have altered its structure. Second, is the fascinating series of fissures on the Northeast Dome which provide a good look at what happens to a brittle sheet of lava that has been rapidly warped upward. Third, is the total unusual nature of the central crater complex. It is so complicated and atypical that geologists cannot agree as to how such a place was originally formed.

The region also offers great potential for someday providing geothermal energy to Oregon. Even though no hot springs or other such hydrothermal activity has yet been discovered, recent volcanic activity leads geologists to believe that there must be some sort of accessible energy in the area.

This is an interesting place to explore, and there are many trails crisscrossing the entire volcanic field. A visit to Diamond Craters can help instill a better understanding and appreciation of the geological history of Oregon and volcanism in general.

Central vent complex, Diamond Crater
(courtesy of Oregon Dept. of Geology and Mineral Industries)

DIAMOND CRATERS

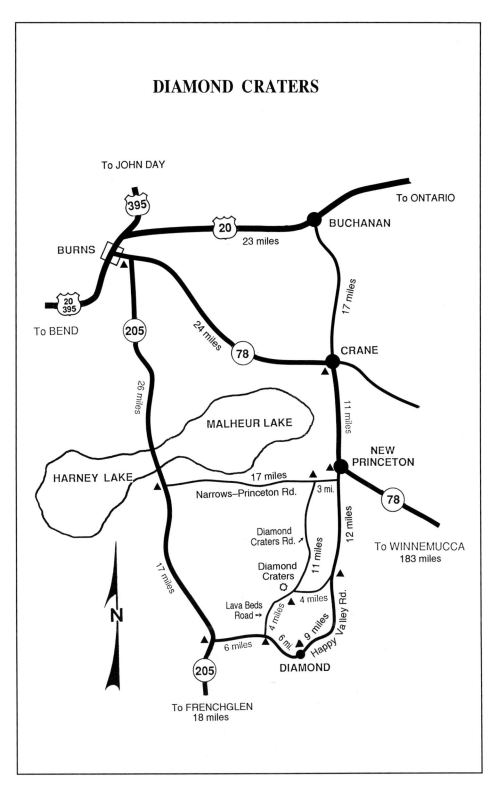

Wonderstone and basanite, a black and gray variety of jasper, can be found at these two locations. Site "A" boasts the basanite, which is procured from the streambed paralleling the highway, as shown on the accompanying map, as well as in Pine Creek, near where Pine Creek Road crosses. Some of the basanite is of a fairly good quality, but it takes some searching to find the best. Be certain to pull well off the highway. There aren't too many adequate places to pull off, so be on the lookout for good places as you approach milepost 156. It is possible to walk along the creekbed for quite a distance in either direction to search for large chunks of basanite.

The mineral of most interest in this region, however, is not basanite. It is an unusually colorful variety of rhyolite known as wonderstone. This interestingly patterned material is found at Site "B," not far from the large Grange Hall. The best is filled with bands and swirls, some of which is solid enough to take a fairly good polish. As was the case with the basanite, the wonderstone occurs in a wide range of qualities, and sufficient time should be allocated to obtain the best the site has to offer.

Park next to the road cut, at the given mileage, and carefully examine as much rhyolite as possible. It is helpful to split stones to better ascertain their color saturation and patterning. Dipping freshly exposed surfaces in water helps to more accurately determine quality. This interesting material occurs in shades of red, rust, orange, brown, green, and beige, and can be used to make larger polished pieces, including bookends, clock faces and even big cabochons. The wonderstone deposit is extensive, but much is on private property. Be sure to only explore regions immediately adjacent to the roadway, or seek permission to explore the private areas ahead of time.

Parked at Site "B"

BUCHANAN

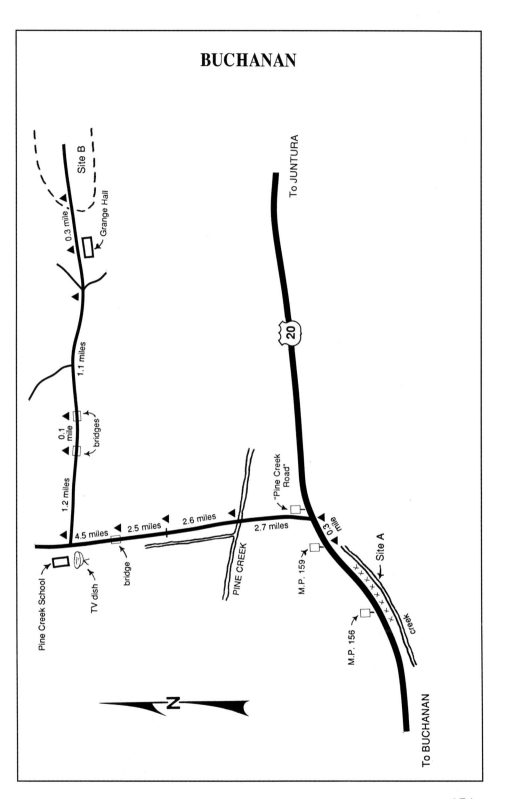

To JUNTURA

20

Site B

0.3 mile

Grange Hall

1.1 miles

0.1 mile

bridges

1.2 miles

4.5 miles

2.5 miles

2.6 miles

2.7 miles

"Pine Creek Road"

0.3 mile

M.P. 159

Site A

M.P. 156

PINE CREEK

creek

bridge

TV dish

Pine Creek School

N

To BUCHANAN

131

Interesting fossil leaf prints and plentiful agate and jasper can be found at these two sites. To get to them, follow the ruts leading north off Highway 20 between milepost 166 and milepost 167. Be advised that they are not easy to spot, but are directly opposite a major ranch road. Once off the pavement, the going is somewhat rough and a small stream must be crossed a couple of times, making it mandatory to have a rugged vehicle, preferably equipped with four-wheel drive.

Site "A" is easy to spot, being composed of bright white cliffs, just west of the road. It is in this white chalky material that one finds the leaf prints. The prints are not easy to find, but they are fun to look for. Simply break off some of the white material and look for brown or black markings, those designating a leaf layer. At that point, start splitting. Once a portion of a print is spotted, be extremely careful when trying to fully expose it, since the host rock is fairly fragile and one wrong placement of a chisel could destroy the delicate prints. It takes patience to obtain complete prints, but the specimens you do find should make the effort worthwhile. It is also possible to find black dendrites on the bright white host rock, and such specimens also can be used to make interesting display pieces.

Site "B" is widespread, extending throughout the little hills. Park anywhere within the given mileage and walk through the hills with a collecting bag. Most of the jasper and agate is found on the upper slopes, but some can be picked up from lower areas. Colors range from white to black and include orange, red, green and yellow, often filled with interesting inclusions. Some tend to be fairly dull, so take time to locate material with the brightest colors and best patterns. Be on the lookout for snakeskin agate and rhyolite; some of the latter is colorful and has interesting markings.

*White
Cliffs*

WHITE CLIFFS

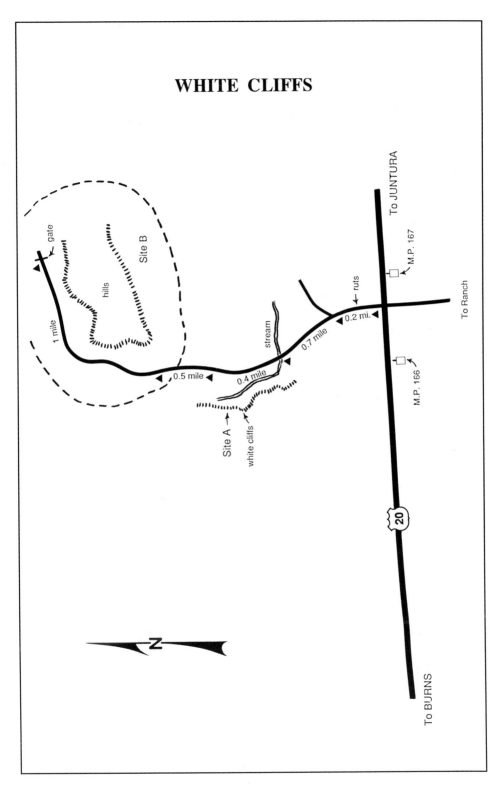

The petrified wood found at this location is highly regarded for its faithful replication of the internal cell structure, external appearance, and often beautiful internal color. The oak specimens are generally the most highly prized, but anything found here should be of an especially high quality. This is a vast collecting area, with petrified and opalized logs being found in a belt about twenty miles long lying along the eastern ridges of Stinkingwater Mountain.

To get there, proceed east on Highway 20 from milepost 167 about six-tenths of a mile and then turn right onto the well-graded dirt road. Drive six miles, then turn right one and one-tenth miles, and then left, heading up onto the mesa. The hill to the collecting site is steep, extremely rough, and rocky. A rugged vehicle with good clearance is essential. When on the mesa, there is no particular place to stop. Due to the roughness of the road, you will want to stop shortly after reaching the summit. Some wood can be found just lying on the surface. To get the largest and best specimens, you will probably have to do some tough digging. You will see pits left by previous rockhounds, those being good indicators where to start.

The digging is not especially easy here, in fact it is very difficult. There is plenty to be found, with sizes ranging from tiny chips to colossal logs. A pick, shovel, and gloves are mandatory, and other hard rock tools might also come in handy when trying to remove the wood from the surrounding basalt. Be sure to pay close attention to all stones you come across while carrying out your excavation work, to ascertain whether you have hit wood, or more of the abundant host rock. If you do not feel like doing such hard work or are not sure your vehicle can make it, good specimens can also be found in nearby Clear Creek. Simply follow the creek as it winds its way along, keeping an eye out for chunks of petrified wood. Outstanding pieces can be obtained this way, and the best part is that no digging is necessary. In addition, be sure to search any other areas of erosion, since all offer good potential for finding pieces of the prized Stinkingwater wood.

It should be also noted that plenty of agate, jasper and common opal is available here, especially in the basin drained by Clear Creek.

STINKINGWATER WOOD

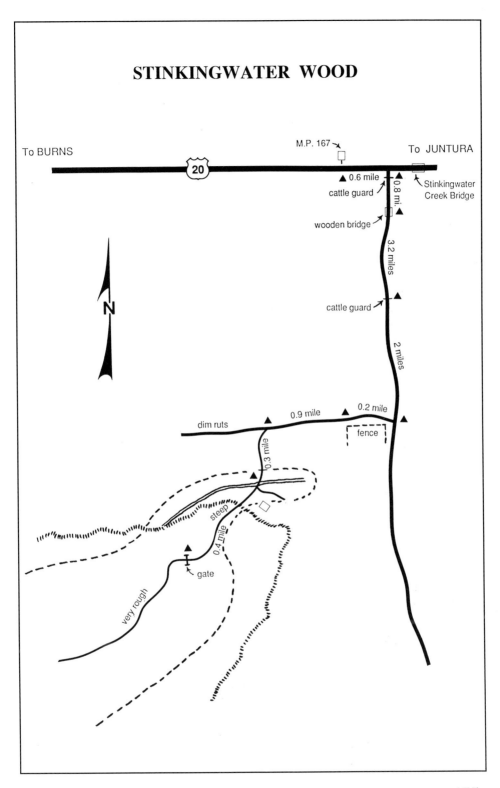

To BURNS

20

M.P. 167

To JUNTURA

▲ 0.6 mile
cattle guard

Stinkingwater
Creek Bridge

0.8 mi.
▲

wooden bridge

3.2 miles

cattle guard ▲

2 miles

dim ruts ▲ 0.9 mile ▲ 0.2 mile ▲

fence

0.3 mile

▲

steep

0.4 mile

▲

gate

very rough

N

This collecting site boasts nice agate, jasper and petrified wood and is conveniently located only a short distance off Highway 20. Don't be deceived, however, since the final eight-tenths of a mile takes you over ruts with an extremely high center, making it mandatory to have a high clearance, rugged vehicle. That final stretch parallels the power lines, and, because of that, makes the route easy to find.

The turnoff from Highway 20 is about two-tenths of a mile east of milepost 171, and is fairly easy to spot due to a gate in the fence just off the pavement. In addition, you should be able to spot the remnants of an old mine, on the north, situated in the center of the collecting site. The best region for collecting tends to be on the slopes of the conspicuous butte overlooking the mine. Agate, jasper and occasional chunks of petrified wood can be found scattered just about anywhere in the region. Material can even be picked up along the power line road.

The quality and quantity vary considerably here, so some patient exploration of the environs is essential to guarantee you will be able to find the best the site has to offer. It is a pleasant place to search. Pay particularly close attention to ravines and other areas of erosion, and hike onto the lower slopes of the butte. Most of the agate is white and filled with interesting inclusions, primarily being a type of bog agate, much of which can be used to produce unusual and interesting polished pieces. Sizes range from small pebbles to fist size, with the majority tending to be somewhat small.

Remnants of mine at collecting area

JUNTURA

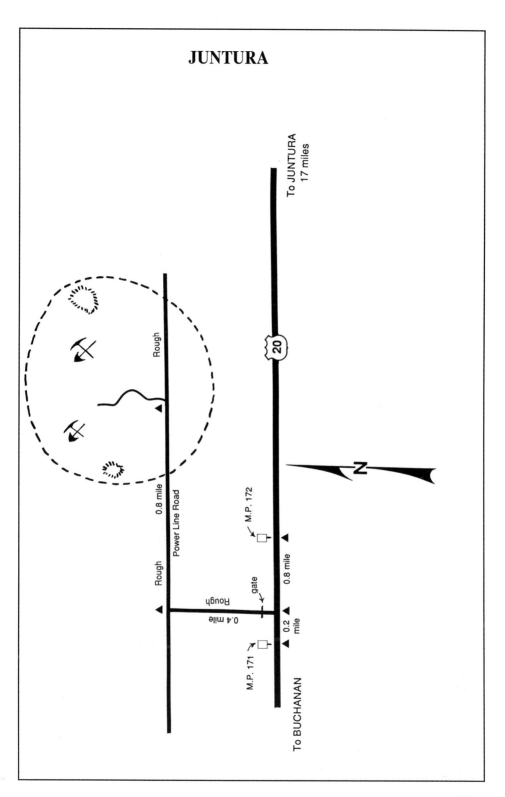

To JUNTURA
17 miles

20

N

Rough

0.8 mile

Power Line Road

Rough

M.P. 172

gate

Rough

0.4 mile

0.8 mile

0.2 mile

M.P. 171

To BUCHANAN

137

These three sites offer a wide range of collectibles, including agate, jasper, chalcedony, and petrified wood. Each location is quite extensive and, within each, the quality and quantity of what can be found varies greatly. Be sure to allow sufficient time to adequately explore them.

At Site "A," agate, jasper, and chalcedony can be found on both sides of the road, but concentrations are sporadic. If you find little or nothing on your first try, simply move on to another spot. The best collecting seems to be on the west side of the road, past the gate. Dimensions tend to be somewhat small, but fist-size chunks of agate and jasper are not rare, especially as you get away from the main road. Colors are predominately orange and yellow, but occasional pieces of green jasper can be found near the mounds on the east side of the main road.

Outstanding black dendritic agate, white plume agate and some colorful jasper can be picked up. Look along the shoreline and throughout the hills and ravines at the southern end of the Warm Springs Reservoir, designated as Site "B." Occasional chunks of spectacular red plume agate can be found. Park and hike through the hills. Like at Site "A," the concentrations and quality vary considerably. At Site "C," petrified wood can be obtained. Most is on the hill just west of the road. Additional chunks can be picked up for a distance, in all directions. The wood is not too spectacular, but some shows its original grain and exterior structure, making good display pieces. A few will take polish, but most are only specimen grade. The best material is obtained by digging into the side of the little hill with a pick and shovel.

A selection of agate, jasper and chalcedony from the collecting sites

WARM SPRINGS

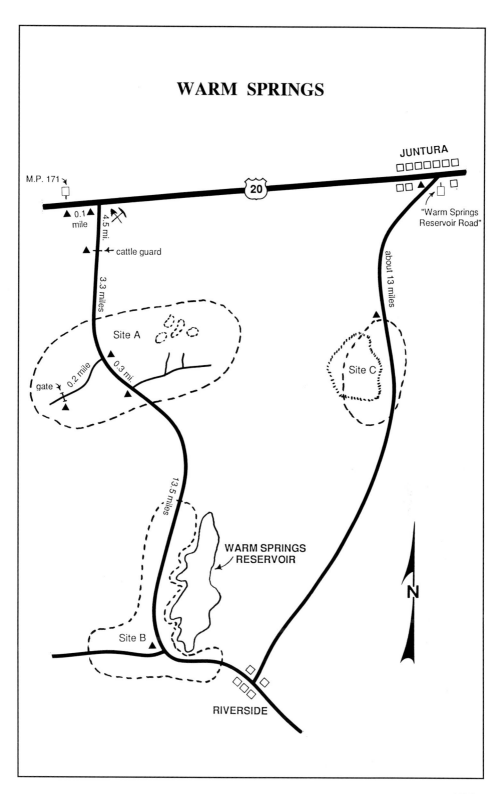

JUNTURA

M.P. 171

US 20

▲ 0.1 mile

4.5 mi.

▲ ← cattle guard

3.3 miles

Site A

gate ↓ 0.2 mile ▲ 0.3 mi. ▲

"Warm Springs Reservoir Road"

about 13 miles

Site C

13.5 miles

WARM SPRINGS RESERVOIR

N

Site B ▲

RIVERSIDE

The two locations illustrated on the accompanying map offer collectors an opportunity to find Pliocene plant and animal fossils. Be advised that the author has had minimal luck at both spots and they are presented only because other reliable sources indicate the visit might be worthwhile to anyone having an interest in such fossils.

To get to Site "A," go east from Burns on Highway 20 about forty-six miles. Eight-tenths of a mile before reaching milepost 177 at Drinkwater Pass, the highway passes by a series of white road cuts on the north. It is within those road cuts and, more specifically, in the rubble at their base, where collectors can find the fossils. Carefully examine suspect rock for any traces of fossil shell or plant. Once you find a few specimens, look for similar rock to increase your chance of locating more. The best collecting tends to be within the darker rock rather than the lighter chalky material. Do not allow anything to roll onto the pavement while working here.

As mentioned earlier, do not get your hopes up. The fossils are delicate, small, and much the same color as the host material, making them difficult to find and not particularly spectacular for display in a collection. This location is primarily of interest only to those with a profound academic curiosity in Oregon fossils. If you choose to collect at Drinkwater Pass, be very careful when crossing the busy highway and be certain to park well off the pavement. Vehicles move fast through this pass and no one will be expecting to meet a pedestrian. For the same reason, do not slow below the normal flow of traffic as you search for the site or a good place to park. It may be safer to actually pass through, look for a good spot to pull off, and then double back. Another similar site for fossils of the same time period, labeled Site "B," is also within a road cut about five miles farther east on Highway 20. Find a good place to pull off the pavement, being careful of the road conditions, and search the road cut, remembering the safety warnings.

Drinkwater Pass

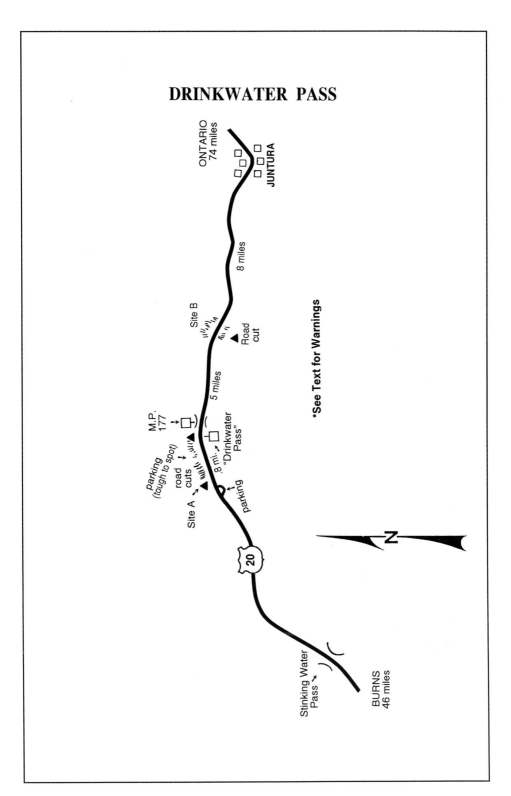

DRINKWATER PASS

ONTARIO
74 miles

JUNTURA

8 miles

Site B

Road
cut

*See Text for Warnings

5 miles

M.P.
177

Parking
(tough to spot)

road
cuts

"Drinkwater
Pass"

.8 mi.

Site A

parking

20

N

Stinking Water
Pass

BURNS
46 miles

141

The region near the southern edge of Beulah Reservoir, about midway between Ontario and Burns, offers rockhounds an opportunity to gather some interesting fossilized leaf prints. Start in Juntura, which is situated on Highway 20 seventy-four miles west of Ontario and sixty miles east of Burns. Just west of town is Beulah Road. This is where you should turn north and continue fifteen miles to the reservoir. There is a sign at the intersection, making the turnoff easy to find.

Just after crossing over the dam, turn left onto Agency Mountain Road and, primarily on the left, are some chalk-like hills. It is within those hills that the very delicate leaf prints can be found. Simply pull well off the road and carefully split the chalky material, paying very close attention for indications of the leaf prints. This location requires that collectors exhibit much patience and care, since it is very difficult to fully expose the prints without damaging them. Once you spot part of a leaf print, it is suggested that you retain the entire rock and finish removing the covering material when at a place more conducive to such delicate and fine work. Use small chisels and awls or ice picks to gently expose as much of the leaf print(s) as possible. Chunks showing many leaves, either partially or fully exposed, can make nice display pieces, but such specimens are not easy to find.

This is definitely a location for collectors with plenty of patience, skill, and a willingness to spend some time.

BEULAH RESERVOIR

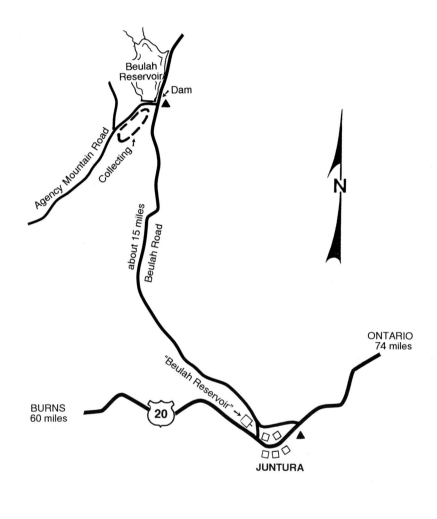

Beulah Reservoir

Dam

Agency Mountain Road

Collecting

about 15 miles

Beulah Road

N

ONTARIO
74 miles

"Beulah Reservoir"

BURNS
60 miles

20

JUNTURA

Excellent specimens of petrified wood can be obtained throughout the slopes of Sourdough Mountain, about 23 miles southwest of Vale. Entire trees have been dug from the rhyolite powder a few feet below the surface gravel. In addition, beautiful blue and yellow limb casts can also be found.

To get to Sourdough Mountain, go west from Vale on Highway 20 about one mile, turn south on the airport road and, after having gone about three miles, turn right onto Sand Hollow Road. Continue another six miles, turn left onto Rock Canyon Road, travel eleven miles, and from there, prominent Sourdough Mountain can easily be seen. Turn right one-half mile and then left about one more mile to the eastern foothills.

There is no exact spot to start digging. Search for pits and areas of excavation where previous rockhounds have been before. Carefully sift through rubble and soil in and around those diggings looking for fragments of the often colorful wood and limb casts to get an idea what can be found. In addition, such excavations should provide a good starting point for your work.

This site is best explored in a four-wheel drive vehicle, since it is necessary to follow the tracks leading toward and around the mountain, some of which are very rough and, occasionally, impassable even with a high-clearance four-wheel drive unit. Do not venture into areas your vehicle was not intended to go. Either hike or be satisfied with what can be found near the main road.

This is one of those places where you can hit the jackpot and find a buried treasure or you can dig for days and not strike much of anything. Again, look for clues on the surface in the form of chips or small pieces and don't just jump out of the car and start digging. A pick and shovel are essential, as are a good pair of gloves and the willingness to do some hard work. Pack lots to drink, since the dry climate can be dehydrating.

There is some private property in the area, and you should not trespass without first gaining permission to do so. In addition, be advised of government restrictions related to the collection of petrified wood, as mentioned earlier in the book.

VALE WOOD

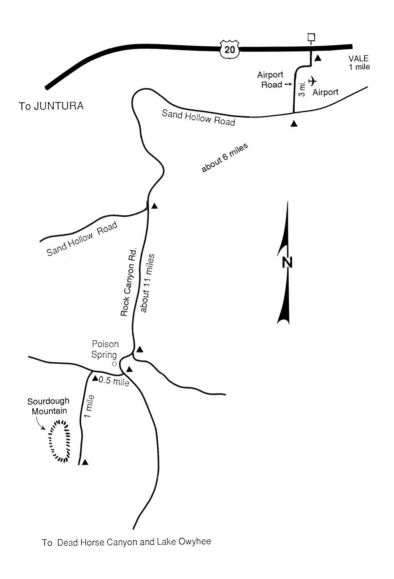

To JUNTURA

20

Airport
Road →

3 mi. ✈ Airport

VALE
1 mile

Sand Hollow Road

about 6 miles

Sand Hollow Road

Rock Canyon Rd.

about 11 miles

N

Poison
Spring

▲0.5 mile

Sourdough
Mountain

1 mile

To Dead Horse Canyon and Lake Owyhee

Some of the most colorful and unusual forms of agate and jasper obtainable anywhere in Oregon are found here. The site is not too difficult to find, and the roads are not bad, except for the final one-half mile stretch, which is a steep climb onto a mesa. A rugged vehicle is recommended for the trip, and essential for the final half mile. If you do not think you can make that final climb, simply park below and hike up. While walking, you will spot abundant fine cutting material, but save it for the trek back.

The journey begins in Owyhee, where you should take Owyhee Avenue west out of town five and eight-tenths miles to Oxbow Basin Road. Turn left, travel one-half mile to the fork, bear right, continue four and eight-tenths miles, turn to the left and go another two and three-tenths miles. At that point, turn left, continue nine-tenths of a mile, and then take the steep and rough ruts leading left onto the mesa for approximately one and one-tenths miles.

At the collecting site the ground is covered with pits, indicating where previous rockhounds have dug before. This region of prime mineral concentration is about three-tenths of a mile BEFORE the summit and road's end. Collecting extends along the ridge for quite a distance, and the variety is incredible. For that reason, be sure to allow enough time to properly sample as much of the area as possible. There is beautiful lace agate and jasper, some incredibly colorful swirled and flow material, in shades of yellow, orange, gold and brown. Even excellent picture and polka-dot jasper available. In addition to the seemingly limitless color and pattern combinations, there are a large number of single hue jasper and agate representing just about any color imaginable, including a nice jade-green variety.

Good material can be found as float, especially near the old burrows and pits, but the very best and largest specimens are usually obtained by doing some digging. For that reason, it is suggested you have a pick and shovel, along with a good rock hammer. To determine exactly where to start work, examine the rubble around as many of the existing pits as you can, to get a good idea of what was found before. You then can decide which region has the best chance of supplying exactly what you want.

Parked at collecting site

OWYHEE

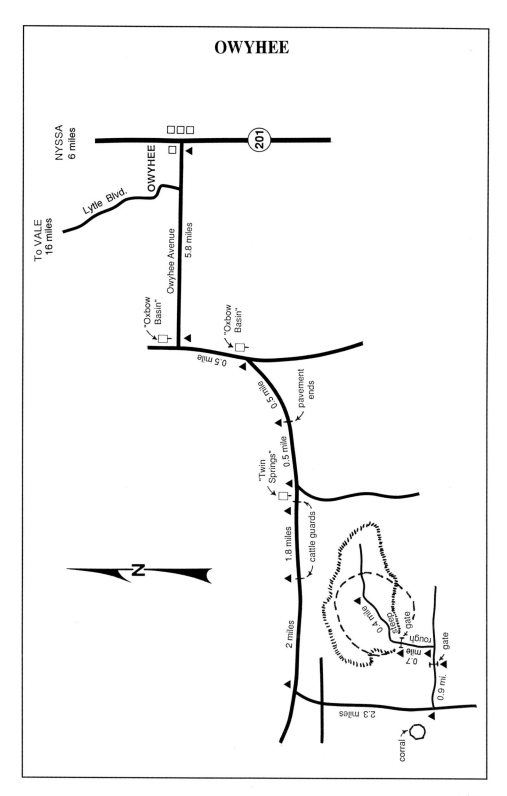

Succor Creek is a well-known source of jasper, agate, nodules, and petrified wood. The name Succor Creek conjures up visions of such localities as Rockville School, McKenzie Ranch, Fenwick Ranch, Owyhee Reservoir and Specimen Ridge. Each is renowned, in its own right, for its fine minerals. Over sixteen types of petrified wood have been identified in the Succor Creek region, and nearly fifty different fossilized shrubs. Most collecting areas are within the boundaries of the Succor Creek State Recreation Area. Rockhounds are free to obtain specimens. Follow a few simple rules which include requests that no commercial collecting be conducted, no digging be done within 500 feet of campgrounds, roads or in archaeological sites, and no explosives be used. Only hand tools can be used to obtain specimens.

The map site shows the most accessible collecting possibility in the southern portion of the Succor Creek area. You may stumble upon other high-quality mineral deposits, especially if you do some exploration on your own. To get to the Succor Creek region from the south, take Succor Creek Road eight and one-tenth miles from where it intersects Highway 95, two and two-tenths miles from the Idaho/Oregon border. At the given mileage you will be at the Rockville School and should bear left, continuing seven-tenths of a mile to where some ruts lead left into the collecting site. The location is easily identified. Some unusual mounds mark the center of a small petrified forest. Colorful jasperized wood is scattered throughout the mound region. Even though this has long been a popular collecting spot, there seems to still be plenty available. Some of the wood is opalized and will take a polish. Be advised that much of the wood is only specimen grade, and too porous and/or crumbly to take a good polish. Pay particularly close attention to areas of erosion on and around the mounds to find the best.

Road leading to Site "A"

SUCCOR CREEK SOUTH

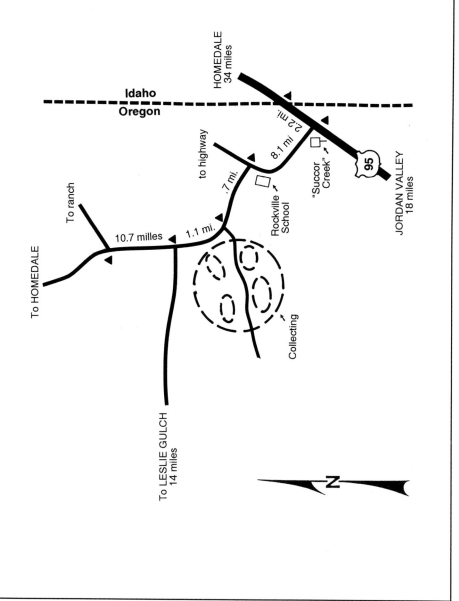

Like Succor Creek South, this region is renowned for fine minerals which include jasper, agate, nodules, and petrified wood. The sites discussed here are the most accessible, but lots more can be found if you are willing to explore on your own. To get to the specific sites, go north on Succor Creek Road eighteen and nine-tenths miles from the Leslie Gulch turnoff, and, at that point, the road to Site "A" will be seen leading off to the right. Site "A" boasts plenty of jasper and agate, including some which is filled with moss-like inclusions. Park anywhere in the region shown on the map and explore the surrounding terrain. From here, continue north for quite a few miles. Just about all roads lead through some sort of agate and/or jasper fields.

At Site "B," you can pick up a good variety of chalcedony, agate and jasper. Dig through the dumps of the old mine or walk along the lowlands to find material that has washed down from higher deposits. If you continue along the road another mile, a trail will be seen leading up the mountain on the right. It is a tough, steep hike to some fairly productive purple agate seams, but the effort might be worthwhile. A sledge hammer and gads will be needed to remove the colorful cutting material from the mountain.

Site "C" is situated at the top of a ridge and occasional specimens of famous Succor Creek Picture Jasper may be found there. Most occur in seams, and hard work is required to remove anything worthwhile. Start by cleaning out holes left by earlier rockhounds in hopes of discovering a good seam which might have been intentionally hidden. Thundereggs can be found throughout the Succor Creek area. They often contain pastelite or agate which is filled with black dendrites, green moss or golden plumes. Be on the lookout for the prized little orbs. Fine opalized wood, as well as all other of the region's collectibles, can be found scattered in and around Succor Creek all the way from Homedale to Rockville. Be sure to allow time for collecting whenever you come across Succor Creek or other regions of erosion.

*Miscellaneous
polished pieces*

SUCCOR CREEK NORTH

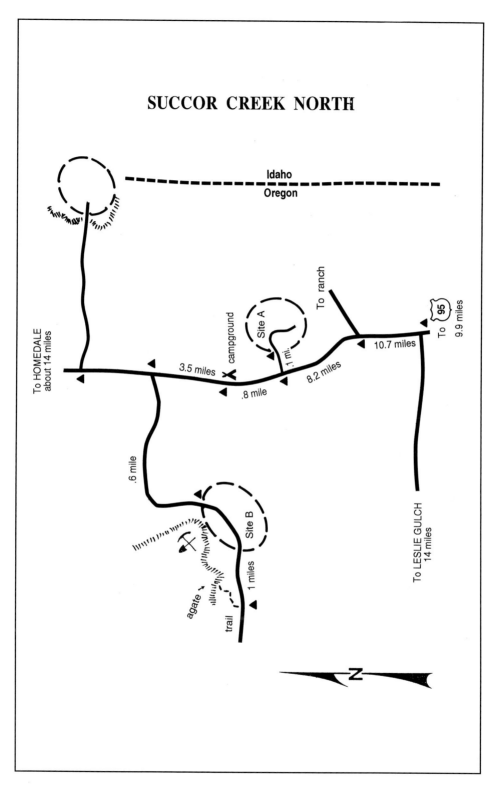

Idaho
Oregon

To HOMEDALE
about 14 miles

campground

Site A

To ranch

3.5 miles

.8 mile

.1 mi.

8.2 miles

10.7 miles

95

To
9.9 miles

To LESLIE GULCH
14 miles

.6 mile

Site B

agate

trail

1 miles

N

These four sites are just east of the Oregon border, in Idaho, and boast petrified wood, opalized wood, bloodstone, jasper, and agate. Site "A" is an extensive location, featuring petrified wood, agate and bright orange jasper. Stop a number of times as you travel along the road within the area designated on the map. The wood tends to be small and is tough to spot, having a color similar to the surrounding soil. Once you find your first piece, others become easier to locate. Material is not too plentiful, but hiking a distance from the road generally provides better and larger specimens.

Site "B" boasts more petrified wood and jasper, but as was the case at Site "A," material is somewhat scarce. This is one of those locations where patient searching is required, but you will be surprised how little time it takes to gather a worthwhile quantity of quality material.The best collecting in this general region is at Sites "C" and "D." The road leading to both is about one-tenth of a mile from the Oregon/Idaho border, as shown on the map. Site "C" offers beautiful green and red moss agate, bloodstone, green jasper with brown dendrites, multicolored jasper in tones of yellow, red and brown, as well as petrified wood. Some opalized wood can also be found here, but it tends to be colorless or gray. Do not hesitate to do some hiking around the little pond, always keeping a keen eye to the ground. Much of the agate at Site "C" has a brownish coating, so any smooth such stones should be cracked to expose the interior, to reveal their true identity.

Site "D" is one of the best opalized wood collecting sites in the territory. The site is in the middle of a little petrified forest and specimen sizes vary from tiny chips to logs. Material is scattered, but appears to be concentrated in certain spots while void in others. When walking through the soft soil, keep an eye out for the bright white chips associated with the beautiful opalized wood. Larger pieces are usually found by digging, so look for previous diggings to determine a good place to start.

Collecting at Site "D"

SOUTH OF HOMEDALE

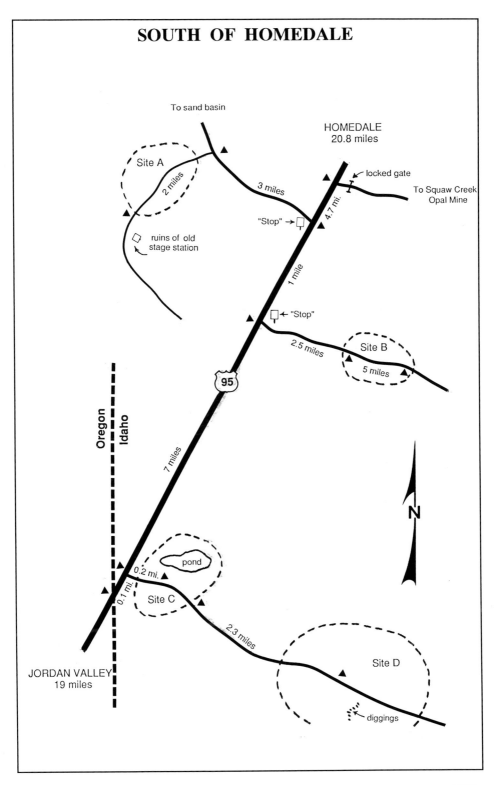

To sand basin

HOMEDALE
20.8 miles

Site A

2 miles

3 miles

locked gate

To Squaw Creek
Opal Mine

"Stop" →

4.7 mi.

☐ ruins of old
stage station

1 mile

☐ ← "Stop"

2.5 miles

Site B

5 miles

95

Oregon
Idaho

7 miles

N

pond

0.2 mi.

0.1 mi.

Site C

2.3 miles

Site D

diggings

JORDAN VALLEY
19 miles

Access to these three locations is from Oregon, but the sites themselves are in Idaho. They feature petrified wood, opalized wood, garnet, cassiterite, and nice quartz crystals. When heading south on Highway 95, the turnoff will be found about one mile before reaching the tiny town of Sheaville. There is a sign designating it to be the road to Silver City and Murphey.

Follow the map to Site "A," which starts about four miles in from the pavement and continues about six more miles on either side of the road. Look for nice pieces of petrified and opalized wood in and around Cow Creek, paying particularly close attention for specimens being eroded out from the soil by the tiny waterway. Digging into the banks is often helpful, but try not to foul the water, since livestock use it for drinking. Additional chunks of wood and nice lace agate can be found on the surrounding hillsides, so be sure to take time to adequately explore as much of the terrain as possible.

At Site "B," search Jordan Creek for garnet and cassiterite pebbles. This location extends all the way to Silver City. Making a few stops for sampling as you continue to Site "C" might prove to be fruitful. It is generally necessary to do a little digging in the streambed to obtain these heavier minerals, since they tend to settle quickly. The work is not difficult, though, and this a pleasant area to spend some time. A sorting screen and washing box would be very helpful here, if you have such equipment.

Nice, but generally small, quartz crystals can be obtained in the mine dumps and hills surrounding the dumps associated with the old Silver City mining region, designated Site "C" on the map. Along with the fine quartz crystals that can be found there, it is also a fascinating place to explore. Some of the old mines may not be abandoned making it necessary not to trespass and to restrict all collecting to regions open for rockhounding.

This area gets fairly hot during the summer months, making it a better winter, spring and fall location.

SHEAVILLE

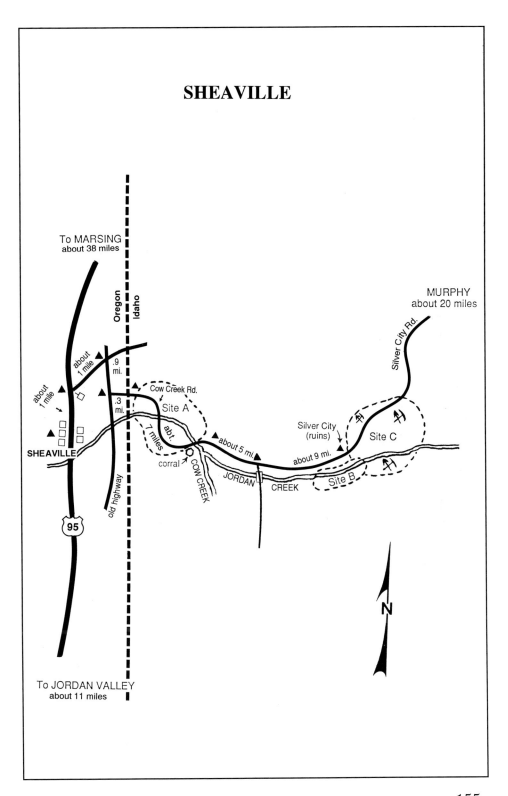

To MARSING
about 38 miles

Oregon | Idaho

MURPHY
about 20 miles

about 1 mile

.9 mi.

about 1 mile

Cow Creek Rd.

Site A

.3 mi.

Silver City Rd.

SHEAVILLE

7 miles

abt.

corral

COW CREEK

old highway

about 5 mi.

Silver City
(ruins)

Site C

about 9 mi.

JORDAN   CREEK

Site B

95

To JORDAN VALLEY
about 11 miles

N

Good specimens of snakeskin agate and Apache tears can be found a short distance from the small town of Rome. To reach there from Highway 95, go east from milepost 60 about eight-tenths of a mile and turn south. The road to the collecting site is very close to the easily spotted large sand pillar, just south of the road, as shown on the map. Be attentive as you approach the given mileage, since it comes up all of a sudden and turning around on this stretch of highway is difficult and somewhat dangerous.

This is a moderately remote collecting site, and not a great place to get stuck. You must cross through some loose sand, thereby making it desirable to have a four-wheel drive vehicle. It is fun to explore, just be properly prepared and do not proceed anywhere your vehicle was not designed to go. The two primary Apache tear fields are easy to identify, since the native soil tends to be considerably lighter. Start picking up the tiny black tears; it won't take long to gather a number of them, and they are great for tumbling. Sizes tend to be small, but a few larger specimens can be found.

The snakeskin agate deposit is situated on some low lying hills just east of the road. There is plenty to be gathered on the surface, but much is weathered and porous. Better pieces can be obtained by digging with a pick and shovel in the soft soil. Occasional chunks of petrified wood can also be found here. The wood tends to be gray and brown and not suitable for polishing, however, some chunks show the wood structure nicely and make great display pieces. The snakeskin agate tends to occur in shade of pale green and yellow, some of which is filled with interesting inclusions. It is easy to spot because of its tubular appearance and wrinkled crust.

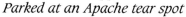

Parked at an Apache tear spot

ROME

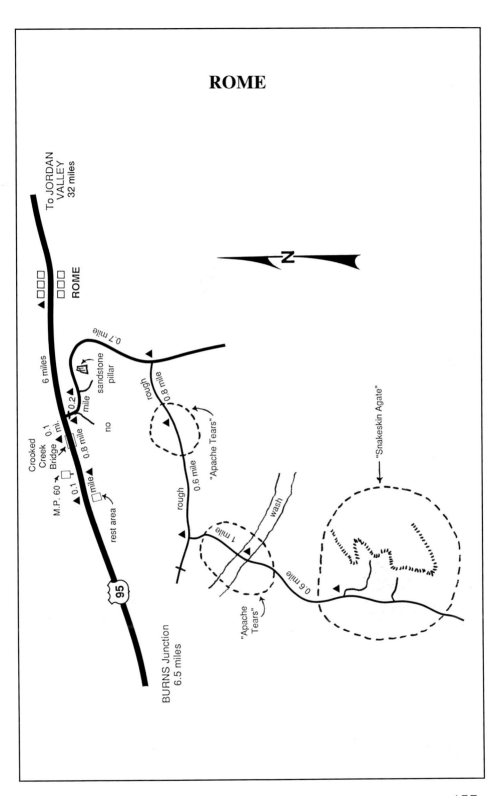

To JORDAN VALLEY 32 miles

ROME

6 miles

0.7 mile

sandstone pillar

0.2 mile

Crooked Creek Bridge

0.1 mi.

no

M.P. 60

0.1

0.8 mile

mile

rest area

95

BURNS Junction 6.5 miles

rough

0.8 mile

"Apache Tears"

rough

0.6 mile

1 mile

wash

"Apache Tears"

0.6 mile

"Snakeskin Agate"

N

157

PETRIFIED WOOD

This is one of Oregon's premier petrified wood locations. The dirt road leading there is well graded and should not present difficulty to most vehicles. Passenger cars could probably make it, if driven very carefully.

The wood location is extensive and plenty of surface material can be found within the region shown on the accompanying map, especially at the now abandoned mine. It is necessary to dig for the largest and best preserved specimen. Hard work is usually rewarded with some of the finest petrified wood Oregon has to offer. Chunks of limbs and even complete tree trunks have been found here, most of which faithfully replicates, in incredible detail, the wood's original structure. Be sure to have a pick, shovel, gloves and a lot of energy, if you decide to do some digging. The entire area is filled with pits where previous rockhounds have worked, and it is suggested you use those excavations as a guide in determining where to start.

This is a prolific location. It takes little effort to gather a quantity of nice petrified wood. Some colorful chunks of agate and jasper can be picked up, so be sure to keep an eye out for those highly desirable collectibles. It is so easy to become overwhelmed by the quality and quantity of the wood, that rockhounds often overlook the beautiful supplementary minerals.

Do not forget the government restricts collectors to gathering no more than 25 pounds of wood per day, with a maximum of 250 pounds in any year. If you unearth a piece weighing more than 250 pounds and would like to see it displayed in a museum or similar institution, a permit for its removal can be requested through the Bureau of Land Management.

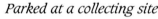
Parked at a collecting site

Mc DERMITT WOOD

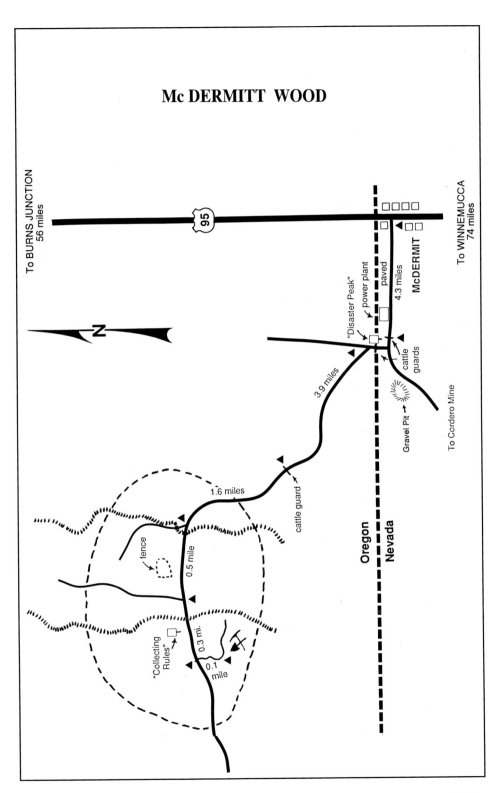

To BURNS JUNCTION
56 miles

95

To WINNEMUCCA
74 miles

N

"Disaster Peak"
power plant

paved
4.3 miles

McDERMIT

cattle
guards

Gravel Pit

To Cordero Mine

Oregon
Nevada

3.9 miles

cattle guard

1.6 miles

fence

0.5 mile

"Collecting
Rules"

0.3 mi.

0.1
mile

159

MINERALS

The three sites illustrated on the map offer rockhounds petrified wood, chert, agate, wonderstone, and jasper. To get to the first, Site "A," go four and three-tenths miles west of town to the Disaster Peak turnoff. Continue right one-tenth of a mile and then left seven and three-tenths miles to a road leading off to the right. Follow that road about seven-tenths of a mile to the center of a collecting area where you can pick up generally small, but frequently well-formed, chunks of petrified wood. In addition, Site "A" offers rockhounds brilliant white chert, agate, and colorful jasper. Pay particularly close attention to areas of erosion, looking for specimens that have been partially uncovered. To find the largest material, you will probably have to do some random digging. If you choose to do so, be sure to refill your holes to prevent injury to cattle and other wildlife.

To get to the next sites, return to the main road and continue west another six and four-tenths miles. Turn right and go through the gate, being sure to close it after passing through. Drive one-tenth of a mile farther, and then follow the ruts up the side of the hill to the easily seen diggings that mark the center of Site "B." Within the region surrounding the quarry one can find abundant swirled rhyolite, often referred to as wonderstone, and opalite, some of which is mixed into the interesting host rock. Good specimens can be extracted from their place in the cliff or from the rubble below. It appears that this quarry has long been abandoned, but if there is any indication otherwise, restrict your search to areas below.

Follow the road, as shown on the map, another one and one-half miles to Site "C." Numerous pits will be seen on both sides of the road, and it is in and around those pits that collectors can gather colorful jasper, petrified wood and banded rhyolite. The wood tends to be gray and tan, but often displays its ancient structure exquisitely. The jasper occurs in a variety of colors, most predominantly orange and red.

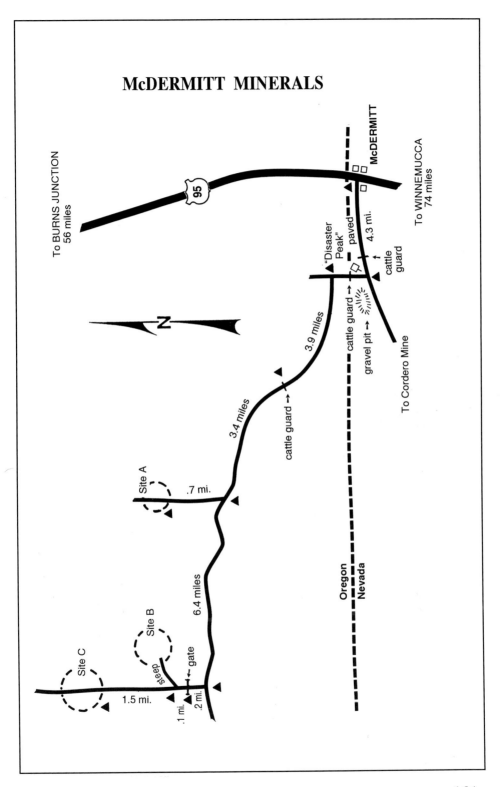

McDERMITT MINERALS

WONDERSTONE

Intricately patterned and banded rhyolite, often referred to as wonderstone, can be found in the hills northwest of McDermitt. To get to the primary collecting site from town, go west four and three-tenths miles to a sign indicating the road to Disaster Peak. At that point, turn north, travel about one-tenth of a mile around the gravel pit, and then proceed left fourteen miles as the road winds its way westward.

As you approach the given mileage, many pits and associated rubble will be seen, primarily on the left. This marks the center of the wonderstone deposit. Look through the various excavations to ascertain exactly what can be found. Either gather wonderstone from the tailings or do some digging directly into the hard rock, extracting material from regions which appear to offer the most potential.

Procuring the tough rhyolite from its place in the ground involves hard work, but the rewards can be well worth the effort. Some of this fascinating stone displays nice scenic "pictures," while other samples are simply filled with bands and swirls. The finest material exhibits very high contrast and will take a dull polish. Be advised that much of what can be found here is very grainy, so it takes a concerted effort to find pieces that will have good lapidary applications. Some of the more porous material, though, is so unusual that it still might be usable for producing larger items such as bookends and clock faces where a quality polish is not mandatory.

There are many mining claims in the general area, so be sure to restrict your collecting to regions outside these claims!

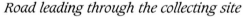

Road leading through the collecting site

McDERMITT WONDERSTONE

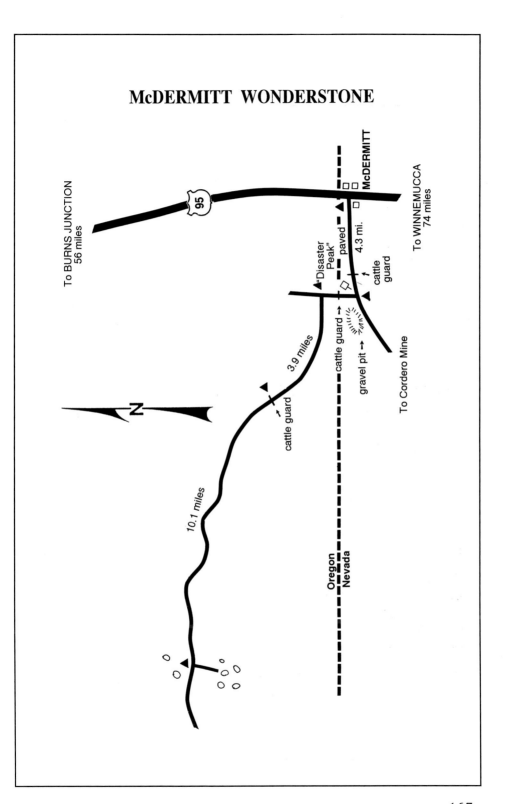

To BURNS JUNCTION
56 miles

95

To WINNEMUCCA
74 miles

McDERMITT

▲"Disaster Peak"

paved

4.3 mi.

cattle guard

cattle guard

gravel pit →

To Cordero Mine

3.9 miles

cattle guard

N

10.1 miles

Oregon
Nevada

Of the more than 150 mining claims staked in the world-famous Virgin Valley, these are the only two that are open to amateur collectors. The valley boasts some of the finest precious opal to be found anywhere, including Australia, and having the opportunity to find specimens of that incredibly colorful gemstone is a dream come true for rockhounds.

To get to the mines, take Highway 140 about twenty-five miles west from Denio Junction to the sign designating the Virgin Valley turnoff. From there, head two and one-half miles south to the campground, bearing left to the Rainbow Ridge Mine, the first of our two stops. Follow the signs to the mine, about five miles farther.

At time of publication the mine was open annually from Memorial Day until Labor Day, and collectors were charged a per person, per day fee to explore the tailings. Collectors at Rainbow Ridge do not dig directly into the opal-bearing strata because of its inaccessibility. Instead, the owner strips away the approximate thirty feet of overburden onto the dumps for collectors. The mine is usually open five days a week, being closed on Tuesdays and Thursdays so the management can replenish the tailings with fresh material. Hours of operation are from 8:00 a.m. until 4:00 p.m. For more information contact them at Box 97, Denio, Nevada 89404, (702) 941-0270.

To reach to the other mine, the Royal Peacock, return to the campground and double back to the left, as shown on the map. At time of publication, the mine was open from the middle of May through the middle of October, from 8:00 a.m. until 4:00 p.m., seven days a week. You can search through the tailings for a reduced fee or attack the opal-bearing clay itself for a higher price. The latter is tough and time consuming work, but the rewards can be substantial.

The Royal Peacock offers full RV hookups and there is a furnished trailer available for rental. If you would like to reserve a space or the trailer, it is suggested that you communicate with the management well ahead of your visit. For further information, contact the Royal Peacock Opal Mine, Inc., at P.O. Box 55, Denio, Nevada 89404, or call (702) 941-0374.

Specimens of native opal are available at each of the mines and it is advisable, whether you plan to buy anything or not, to examine them. Knowing what you are looking for greatly enhances your chances for success. You must also bring your own tools which should include a small garden rake, trowel, spray bottle for water, gloves, hat and sunscreen. In addition, a short-handled pick, shovel, screwdriver, and kneeling pads are suggested.

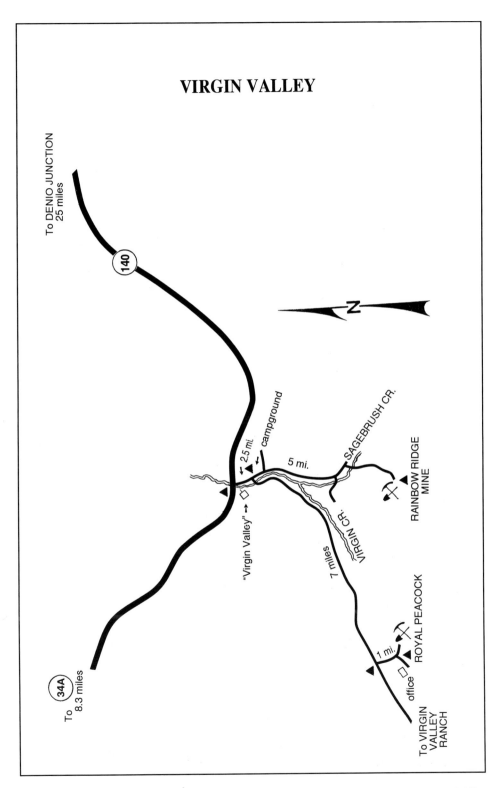

VIRGIN VALLEY

To DENIO JUNCTION
25 miles

140

N

campground

2.5 mi.

SAGEBRUSH CR.

5 mi.

RAINBOW RIDGE
MINE

"Virgin Valley" →

VIRGIN CR.

7 miles

ROYAL PEACOCK

1 mi.

office

To
34A
8.3 miles

To VIRGIN
VALLEY
RANCH

This location is in Nevada, just a few miles southeast of Oregon. The trip will take you through numerous obsidian and Apache tear fields, and even affords an opportunity to encounter herds of wild horses and other interesting wildlife. Four specific sites are discussed, but anywhere along the road provides good collecting possibilities.

Start where Road A-34 intersects Highway 140, about twelve miles southeast of the Oregon state line. Drive onto well-graded Cedarville Road (A-34) and proceed southwest approximately three miles to the start of Site "A." Site "A" boasts an unusually productive concentration of obsidian and Apache tears and it extends at least two more miles on either side of the road. Stop anywhere within the given mileage and gather as much as you desire. Some is more transparent than other, so it takes time to find the best. If you choose to split any specimens to ascertain quality and transparency, be sure to wear protective goggles and gloves. When struck with a hammer, the volcanic glass sends needle-like splinters flying through the air.

Another Apache tear and obsidian field is located about two miles beyond the fork, as shown on the map. This is Site "B" and is also quite extensive. Site "C" is somewhat unusual, featuring an exposed deposit of perlite which contains tiny Apache tears. A hillside of this unique, grayish material will be seen on the left side of the road at the given mileage. Pieces filled with Apache tears partially embedded are very nice for display in a mineral collection. Moonstone is also reported to have been found here, so be on the lookout. To get to Site "D," bear right at the fork just past Site "C," and go about eight more miles. This will place you in the center of another obsidian and Apache tear field which extends at least four more miles. Additional obsidian will be encountered all the way to Cedarville (California).

Site "B"

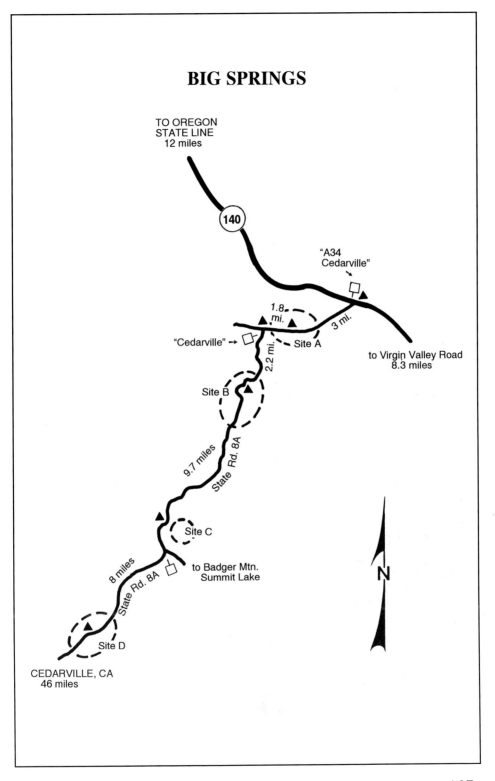

BIG SPRINGS

TO OREGON
STATE LINE
12 miles

140

"A34
Cedarville"

1.8. mi.

"Cedarville" →

Site A

3 mi.

to Virgin Valley Road
8.3 miles

2.2 mi.

Site B

9.7 miles

State Rd. 8A

Site C

to Badger Mtn.
Summit Lake

8 miles

State Rd. 8A

Site D

N

CEDARVILLE, CA
46 miles

This is regarded as one of the premier locations in the entire country for amateur collectors to gather faceting grade sunstones, a gem variety of feldspar. The area is so highly regarded that the Bureau of Land Management has designated it as closed to any type of commercial mining, protecting it for amateur collectors. The roads leading to the area are very good, and just about any vehicle with reasonable clearance should be able to make it in with no trouble. When at the site, there are some primitive toilets, as well as a few picnic tables. Collectors can also spend the night if they wish.

To find the tiny gemstones, walk in any direction and simply pick them up. They are everywhere, and it doesn't take long to gather hundreds. Walk with the sun to your back, since the rays of light will reflect off the glass-like gems making them easier to spot. Most rockhounds crawl on their hands and knees, carrying a cup in which to deposit the little treasures.

Sizes range from small particles to occasional specimens weighing many carats. Obviously the larger ones are the most ardently sought after and, as you might expect, the tougher to find. The most common color tends to be a very light pink. Some, though, can be found with tints of green and red. When faceted, such subtly colored stones are beautiful.

The sunstones can be collected by manual methods only and the B.L.M. prohibits the use of any mechanized equipment or blasting. Also be advised that within the public collecting area there are about twenty acres of private land and five additional private mining claims. You may not collect on those spots without first getting the owner's permission. The boundaries of the public collecting area are identified by sage green triangular signs.

Sign at collecting area

HART MOUNTAIN

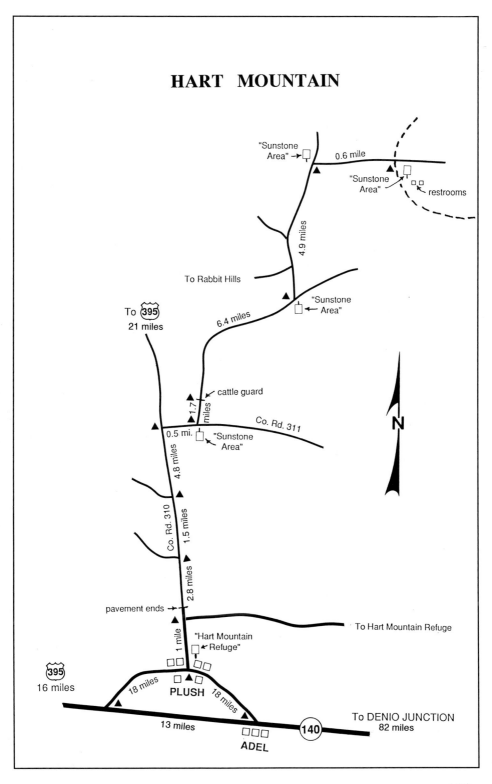

"Sunstone Area" → ▢ 0.6 mile ▲ ▢ "Sunstone Area" → □ □ ← restrooms

4.9 miles

To Rabbit Hills

To (395)
21 miles

6.4 miles ▲ ▢ ← "Sunstone Area"

cattle guard
▲ 1.7 miles

Co. Rd. 311

▲ 0.5 mi. ▢ ← "Sunstone Area"

4.8 miles

Co. Rd. 310 ▲ 1.5 miles

2.8 miles

pavement ends →
▲ 1 mile

To Hart Mountain Refuge

▢ "Hart Mountain
↖ Refuge"

□ □

□ ▲ □
18 miles **PLUSH** 18 miles

(395)
16 miles

▲

13 miles

▲
(140)

□ □ □
ADEL

To DENIO JUNCTION
82 miles

N

Jasper, chalcedony, and petrified wood are abundant throughout the flatlands surrounding Hart Mountain, especially on and near its western slopes. In addition, geodes, thundereggs, fire opal and jasp-agate can also be found. Generally, the nodules and jasp-agate are best obtained in the mountain canyons, while the opal is found high on the nearly inaccessible upper peaks of the western rim. The best way to search this somewhat vast area is to start in the flatlands, looking for higher than usual concentrations of material, and then hiking to any adjacent canyons or foothills, hoping to come upon more plentiful and sizable pieces.

The prime collecting is done within the boundaries of Hart Mountain National Antelope Refuge, and digging or blasting is not allowed. You can gather rocks from the surface. It is an interesting place to explore, affording picturesque landscape, wildlife, and fine minerals. Drive along the main road or any of the other lesser maintained roadways and stop from time to time to ascertain what can be found. Just about any place you spot good concentrations of rock or gravel offers a chance for finding something worthwhile.

One especially productive area is reached by starting at the Refuge Headquarters and driving about five miles northeast toward Frenchglen. At that point, a rough little road leads off to the right to Flook Lake and Black Canyon. If you have a rugged vehicle, follow it a short distance until it enters the lake bed. The lake is dry most of the year, but if it appears to be muddy, proceed with caution or park before going any farther. Plenty of good material can be gathered from easily spotted gravel deposit scattered throughout the barren terrain. Just randomly park and start walking.

It is important to note that there is a rockhounding limit of seven pounds per person per day! In addition, it is illegal to remove any type of Indian artifact from the Refuge.

PLUSH

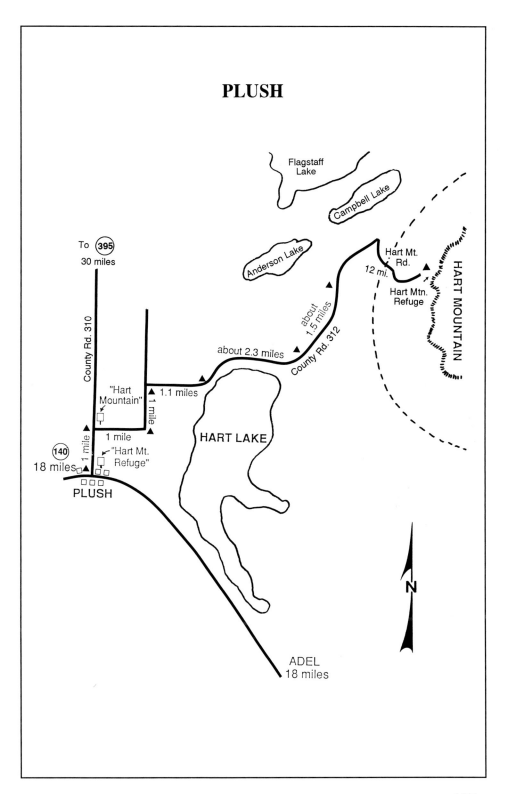

Flagstaff Lake

Campbell Lake

To (395)
30 miles

Anderson Lake

Hart Mt. Rd.

12 mi.

Hart Mtn. Refuge

HART MOUNTAIN

County Rd. 310

about 1.5 miles

about 2.3 miles

County Rd. 312

"Hart Mountain"

1.1 miles

1 mile

1 mile

HART LAKE

(140)
18 miles

1 mile

"Hart Mt. Refuge"

PLUSH

N

ADEL
18 miles

171

Thundereggs can be found in scattered deposits throughout a region stretching south from Lakeview all the way into California. One of the most accessible deposits is shown on the accompanying map. Before heading in, be sure you are in a rugged vehicle, since it is necessary to cross some shallow streams, travel through sand, and climb two steep and somewhat rough stretches of road along the way. Four-wheel drive is probably not essential, but desirable.

To get there, go south from Lakeview three and six-tenths miles on Highway 395. At that point, there is a large house on the right and Crane Creek Road leading off to the left. Turn onto Crane Creek Road and continue three miles to where tracks can be seen on the right going up the hill. Turn, go another mile, bear left at the fork, and continue one-half mile to where a faint trail heads off on the right, that being the route to the thunderegg deposit. There are two large tree stumps, one on each side of the road, indicating where to park. Pull off, and, due to the steep terrain, make certain your parking brake is set firmly before you start the short hike.

The trail is tough to see, due to overgrowth and pine needle build-up, but, if you can't find it, simply head in the general direction shown on the map for about one hundred yards, keeping an eye out for pits made by previous rockhounds. It is necessary to dig for the thundereggs here, so be sure to take along a pick and shovel. For more information about other nearby thunderegg and agate collecting localities, inquire at the Lakeview Chamber of Commerce.

A "clutch" of thundereggs

CRANE CREEK

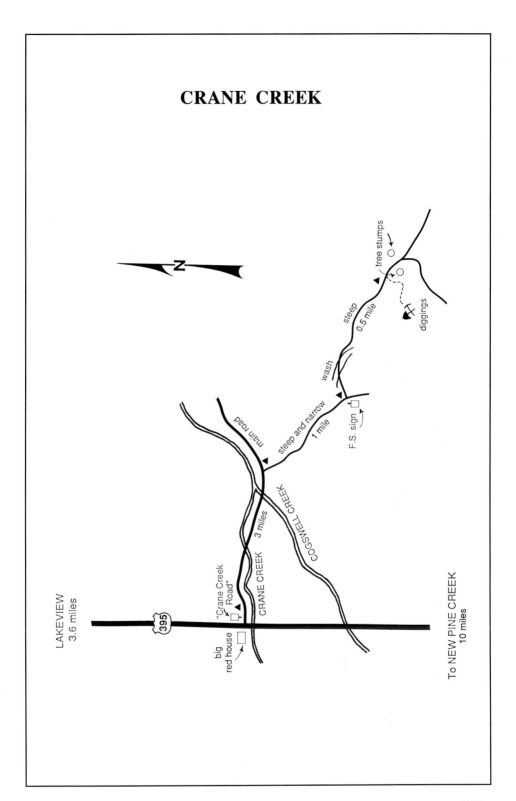

N

LAKEVIEW
3.6 miles

395

"Crane Creek Road"

big red house

CRANE CREEK

3 miles

COGSWELL CREEK

main road

steep and narrow

1 mile

F.S. sign

wash

steep

0.5 mile

tree stumps

diggings

To NEW PINE CREEK
10 miles

173

This remote location offers an opportunity to find occasional thundereggs and geodes. Make note that getting there involves a long and desolate trip. Unless you are very lucky or persistent, the material may not be worth the effort. The site is mentioned only because it has been known to produce nice specimens and is relatively unexplored.

To get there, take Highway 78 to the Fields turnoff, which is twenty-six miles northwest of Burns Junction. Go southwest on Fields-Denio Road about forty miles to Pike Creek, as illustrated on the accompanying map. The road crosses Pike Creek near the northern part of the Alvord Desert and it is within the banks of that creek where the elusive, but often nice thundereggs and geodes, can be found. Inspect regions of erosion near the road or hike a distance along Pike Creek, in either direction.

For the best chance of locating anything worthwhile, dig near where you find chips or portions of thundereggs or geodes. Locating anything worthwhile is a matter of luck and perseverance, since it seems that occurrence is somewhat random. Due to the inaccessibility of this location, there hasn't been much rockhounding done here. That implies that there could be a good potential for finding something significant to those willing to spend the time and effort. If you do choose to visit, be sure to let someone know where you are going, have plenty of fuel and take extra supplies, especially spare water. You will need digging tools, including a pick and shovel, and even a sturdy rake might come in handy. In addition, don't forget some gloves and sun protection. Do not attempt the trip in anything but a rugged vehicle.

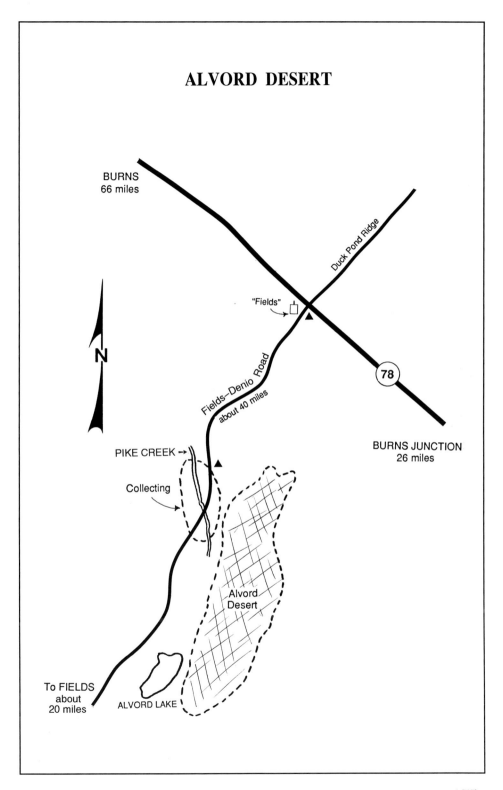

ALVORD DESERT

BURNS
66 miles

Duck Pond Ridge

"Fields"

N

Fields–Denio Road
about 40 miles

78

BURNS JUNCTION
26 miles

PIKE CREEK →

Collecting

Alvord
Desert

To FIELDS
about
20 miles

ALVORD LAKE

175

INTRODUCTION TO
OREGON BEACH COLLECTING

Oregon beaches have gained a certain amount of renown as a result of the beautiful minerals and fossils that are often washed up on the shores. Over twenty distinctly different varieties of agate and jasper have been reported being found on the beaches of Oregon. The greatest quantities of gems are usually found during the winter months, especially after severe storms. Some beaches tend to be more prolific than others, but concentrations from time to time can change. On one day a beach may be filled with colorful agates and jaspers, and shortly after, little or nothing of interest will be left. Just about all Oregon beaches offer the potential for providing specimens of agate, jasper, petrified wood, and fossilized sea life. Those discussed on the following pages proved to be more consistent sources of such collectibles over the years.

The best time to hunt for beach material is as the tide is going out. Not only is it safer then, but the little pebbles are freshly washed and much easier to spot. When you visit any beach always be careful, especially if wading out to rocky reefs or isolated gravel bars. Avoid entering the water if the surf is heavy, no matter how promising an outcrop might appear. If collecting at low tide, do not get yourself trapped somewhere as the tide comes back in. If you use good judgment and are careful, the beaches of Oregon can supply beautiful mineral specimens and hours of collecting pleasure.

In general, the northern beaches contain more jasper, including a nice green bloodstone. As you travel down the coast, agates seem to become more plentiful. Also note that nearly every gravel bar situated where a stream or river enters the ocean offers a better than average chance for finding colorful gemstones.

Typical
Oregon
Beaches

There are numerous beaches along the Oregon coast where a rockhound can find minerals of interest. Those west of Tillamook seem to offer a little more than average, especially the region centered around Netarts and Oceanside. The list of what can be found in the Tillamook area is extensive and features fossils, a beautiful green grossularite garnet, jasper and agate.

To reach to Region "A," take 3rd Street west from Main Street (Highway 101) about two miles and, just after crossing over the Tillamook River, turn right onto Bay Ocean Road. Most of the coastline from that point and continuing quite a distance toward Cape Meares offers collecting potential. The seaside cliffs contain a variety of nice marine fossils and are well worth exploring. In addition, there tends to be many fine agate and jasper pebbles mixed in with much of the gravel. Do not be tempted to climb on or dig into the unstable cliffs, since such activity could create a dangerous situation. Be satisfied with what can be found within the rubble down below.

To locate one particularly productive spot, go about five miles along Bay Ocean Road, turn right onto the levee, and park in the parking area. Hike along the trail leading to the shore through the sand dunes. Carefully examine all the gravel for small, but often nice, jasper and agate pebbles. Keep in mind that beach agates and jaspers often appear dull and uninteresting due to their heavily abraded surface. Examine all suspicious stones carefully. Hidden interiors might be beautiful and filled with interesting inclusions and/or patterns.

Region "B" encompasses the entire stretch of beach starting where the Netarts Highway intersects Cape Meares Loop Road and going all the way north past Netarts and Oceanside, almost to Cape Meares. About five miles north of Netarts, there are some massive gravel deposits, which contain good grades of agate and jasper, including sagenite. Near Oceanside, a green occurrence of massive grossularite garnet, known as "Oregon Jade," can be found, as well as some interesting zeolites.

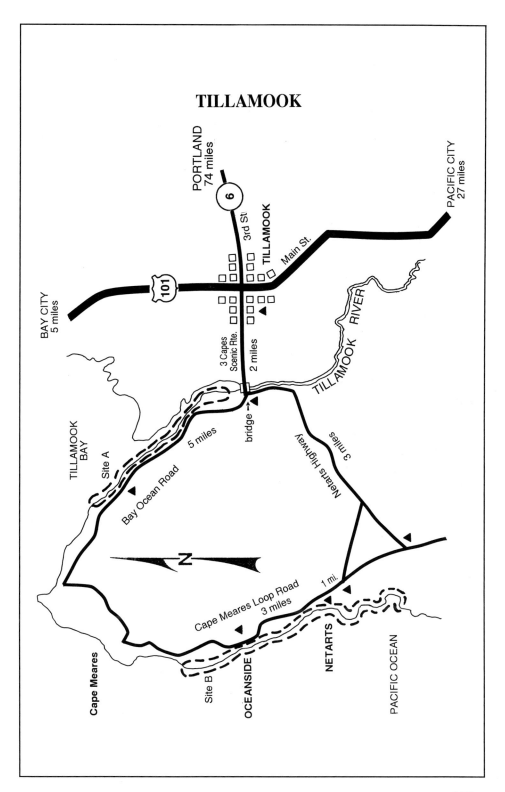

TILLAMOOK

PORTLAND
74 miles

6

3rd St

TILLAMOOK

Main St.

BAY CITY
5 miles

101

PACIFIC CITY
27 miles

TILLAMOOK RIVER

3 Capes Scenic Rte.
2 miles

bridge →

TILLAMOOK BAY

Site A

Bay Ocean Road
5 miles

Netarts Highway
3 miles

N

Cape Meares Loop Road
3 miles

1 mi.

Cape Meares

Site B

OCEANSIDE

NETARTS

PACIFIC OCEAN

Probably the most northern stretch of Oregon coastline of interest to rockhounds is that between Cannon Beach and Cape Falcon. Potentially good collecting can be found just about anywhere between these two points. Accessibility is sometimes difficult. It is usually necessary to explore only those beaches with direct public access such as Arcadia Beach, Tolovana Beach, Hug Point, Cove Beach, and Short Sand Beach.

Any coastline west of Tillamook offers promise, especially at Netarts and Oceanside. This was discussed in the previous section.

Farther south, on the beaches near Lincoln City, excellent specimens of agate, jasper, "Oregon Jade" and even some fossilized coral can usually be found. The Lincoln City beaches are best searched at low tide, since the beautiful agates and jaspers often get trapped in the rocky regions farther out. It is among those rocks where you should concentrate your searching.

From Otter Rock south to Newport, just about any beach will supply pebbles of agate, jasper and petrified wood, as well as an occasional fossilized clam shell. Prime hunting in this area is at Beverly Beach and Agate Beach. Fascinating worm-bored petrified wood has been found on beaches just north of Newport. Potentially good collecting is possible just about anywhere along the shoreline of Yaquina Bay, just south of Newport.

During the winter months, the north side of Waldport Bay is also respected for its fine rockhounding.

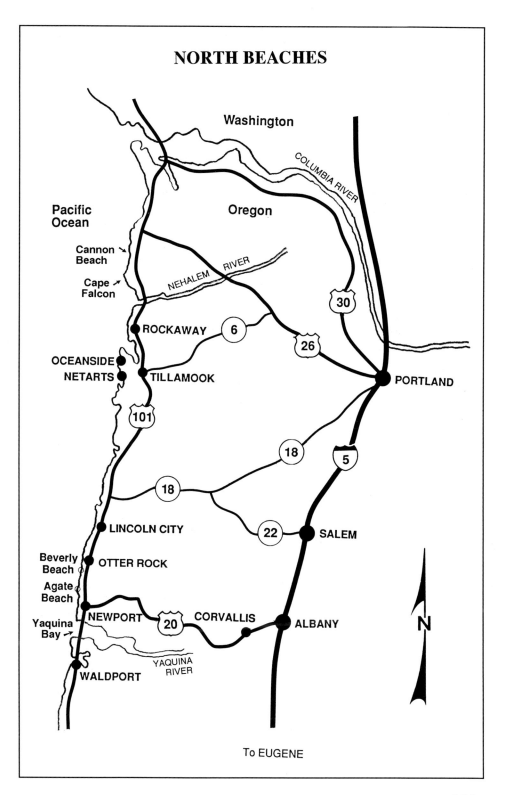

NORTH BEACHES

Washington

Oregon

Pacific Ocean

COLUMBIA RIVER

Cannon Beach

Cape Falcon

NEHALEM RIVER

ROCKAWAY (6)

(26)

(30)

OCEANSIDE

NETARTS

TILLAMOOK

(101)

PORTLAND

(18)

(5)

(18)

(22) SALEM

LINCOLN CITY

Beverly Beach

OTTER ROCK

Agate Beach

NEWPORT (20) CORVALLIS ALBANY

Yaquina Bay

YAQUINA RIVER

WALDPORT

N

To EUGENE

Collecting at beaches near the town of Yachats and extending south to Florence is traditionally among the best in the state. Most of the agate found there contains showy sagenite inclusions, making it a real prize when cut and polished. In addition, petrified wood, chalcedony, bloodstone and a multitude of other colorful varieties of agate and jasper can be found. The prime places to search are where Big Creek and China Creek enter the Pacific Ocean and at Agate Point. Other excellent localities are at the mouth of Tenmile Creek, about eight miles south of Yachats, and at the mouth of Cummings Creek, about three miles south. Washburne Beach is particularly productive, if the tide is low enough to reach the gravel bars.

Farther south, Cape Arago is well respected among collectors. Beautiful multicolored "flower" jasper can be found there, as well as banded agate and petrified wood. Cape Arago is reached from the town of North Bend, north of Coos Bay. Pay particularly close attention to the north and south facing inlets. They generally provide the best collecting opportunities, being positioned better to trap the agate, wood and jasper bearing gravels.

All the beaches in the Coos Bay region are noted for the fine specimens of petrified wood that have been found there.

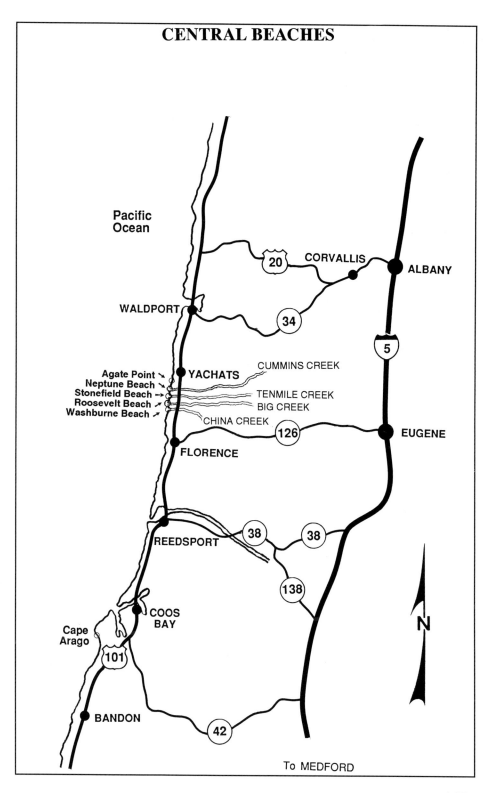

CENTRAL BEACHES

Pacific
Ocean

20 CORVALLIS

ALBANY

WALDPORT

34

5

Agate Point
Neptune Beach
Stonefield Beach
Roosevelt Beach
Washburne Beach

YACHATS

CUMMINS CREEK

TENMILE CREEK

BIG CREEK

CHINA CREEK

126

EUGENE

FLORENCE

REEDSPORT

38

38

138

Cape
Arago

COOS
BAY

101

N

BANDON

42

To MEDFORD

Gem quality agate, jasper, serpentine, "Oregon Jade" (massive grossularite garnet) and petrified wood are the most prolific minerals to be found on the southern Oregon beaches. In addition, always be on the lookout for jade. The jade can occur in shades of pink, white and green, some of which is of high gem quality.

Outstanding specimens of ocean worn agatized myrtle wood, banded agate and "flower" jasper can be picked up on the beach at Seven Devils Wayside, situated midway between Bandon and Charleston.

Nice fossils can be unearthed from the cliffs south of the Cape Blanco lighthouse. The Cape Blanco beaches afford collectors more agate, especially between the mouth of the Sixes River all the way south to Port Orford.

Agate, "Oregon Jade," petrified wood and jasper, in a multitude of colors, can be obtained on most beaches extending north from Gold Beach to Hubbard Mound. Fine specimens of serpentine can be procured in the gravel bars of the Rogue River, also north of Gold Beach. In fact, the serpentine found there is a particularly nice blue-green variety and well worth looking for. It is solid and can be used to produce exquisite carvings and large polished pieces. Carving grade talc can usually be found in and around Gold Beach. The area also boasts occasional chunks of gem quality green jade and some very nice bright red jasper pebbles.

Farther south, at the mouth of the Pistol River, collectors can pick up milky quartz, agate, chert and sporadic pieces of gem quality jade. Look both north and south of where the river enters the Pacific Ocean. Landslides near the Pistol River should also be inspected. Many are caused by the slipping of a nice dark-green serpentine, which can be used for making carvings.

The beaches extending south from Cape Ferrelo to Brookings boast serpentine and grossularite, occurring in shades of green, yellow and red. Good quantities of agate and jasper pebbles can also be found in the gravel bars at and near the mouth of the Chetco River, in Brookings.

SOUTH BEACHES

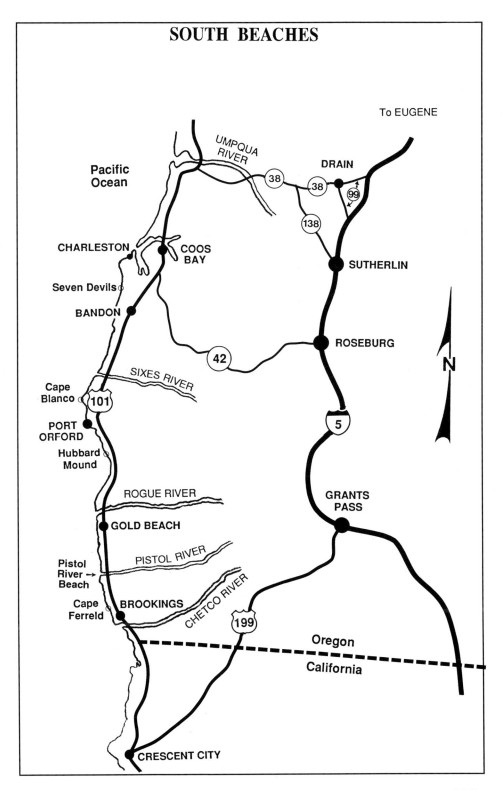

— HINTS FOR COLLECTING MINERALS —

1. Necessary items are prospector's pick, safety goggles, gloves, wrapping materials, hand lens, notebook, pen, hand weeder or hand rake. Your equipment should also include items from the following categories and possibly some of the options.
   - *Shovels:*   Collapsible shovel, spade, miner's shovel
   - *Large picks:*   Miner's pick, 16" ore pick, mattock
   - *Striking tools:*   Crack hammer, chisel point pick, maul, long striking hammer
   - *Chisels:*   Cold chisel, long chisel, wedge, gad, screwdriver
   - *Options:*   Hydraulic jack, screw jack, augers, hand drill, gold pan, gem screens, ultra-violet light, bent wire, paint brush

2. When working in a mine dump look for any mineral which is different from the rest of the pile in color, translucency, shape, luster, or texture.

3. Look for specimens which are combinations of several minerals.

4. Work with someone. When there is heavy digging or rock moving, alternate jobs.

5. Look for cavities in the rock walls.

6. Split large rocks which are composed of several minerals.

7. Look for a contact zone, an area where two different types of rock meet.

8. Micromounts are found in small seams, vugs, old natural fractures, between mica and feldspar plates, and in loose coarse material. Examine all specimens with suspected micromount qualities with a ten-power lens.

9. If you find a good specimen, try to trace where it came from.

10. In any mine or quarry identify the principal rocks, know what minerals may be found with them, and seek out any layer which shows the characteristics you are looking for. Prospect several areas quickly before selecting a place to dig.

11. A water bottle with sprayer is handy on old mine dumps.

12. Investigate the ground around old dumps and old mines.

From Midwest Gem, Fossil and Mineral Trails, Prairie States, by June Culp Zeitner

HINTS FOR COLLECTING GEM MATERIALS

Following are some suggestions for collecting gem materials.

1. Walk back and forth looking at the rocks with the sun in front of you and then behind you. Agates and chalcedony are translucent with the light shining through them. Patterns show off better with the sun be hind you.

2. Look for gemstones after rains if possible. Moisture makes the patterns and color stand out.

3. Learn to check rocks in the field. A small chip can be knocked off from the edge with a prospector's pick by holding the rock firmly with one hand and striking it quickly at the edge with a hard blow. Let your wrist give with the blow.

4. If a rock is already broken, a conchoidal fracture is often a sign it is polishable.

5. Look in streams and along lakes, and also on the grassy hillsides and dirt banks along the lakes and streams.

6. If a rock is of good color but badly fractured, remember your tumbler.

7. Agates may have oxidized coatings. They may also have thumb print depressions or pockmarks.

8. Make a record on the spot of any find you make which is strange or unusual in any way.

9. A spray bottle of water will help determine the characteristics of individual gem materials.

10. The collecting of petrified wood is regulated. You may not take more than 25 pounds in one day or 250 pounds for a year.

From Midwest Gem, Fossil and Mineral Trails, Prairie States, by June Culp Zeitner

ROCKHOUND RULES

The following rules and ethics are to be found in various publications for rockhounds and gem collectors everywhere. Most are obvious and should be observed not only for courtesy to others but also for your own personal safety and pleasure.

1. Tell someone where you are going and when you expect to return.
2. Do not collect alone - have at least one companion and preferably two.
3. Wear appropriate clothing - long pants, work boots, preferably with steel toes, a hard hat if working around vertical rock faces, heavy work gloves and protective eye wear if you are going to be hammering.
4. Research the area you are going to - what kind of vehicle is needed to get there, what is to be found, are there old mine shafts you should be aware of or other dangers, what kind of collecting equipment will you need and be sure to bring a map.
5. Always ask permission to enter property if possible.
6. Leave all gates in the position you found them.
7. Do not disturb livestock.
8. Never, ever litter. If possible, leave the place cleaner than it was when you arrived.
9. Do not "hog" the site or make it difficult for the next person to collect.
10. Do not leave pets or children unattended, they can get into serious trouble.
11. Never leave fires unattended, and do not light them in dry, hazardous conditions.
12. Bring a first aid kit with you.
13. Never enter abandoned mines without proper training, equipment and permission and never alone.

CODE OF ETHICS
The American Federation of Mineral Societies

I will respect both private and public property and will do no collecting on privately owned land without the owner's permission.

I will keep informed on all laws, regulations or rules governing collecting on public lands and will observe them.

I will, to the best of my ability, ascertain the boundary lines of property on which I plan to collect.

I will use no firearms or blasting material in collecting areas.

I will cause no willful damage to property of any kind - fences, signs, buildings, etc.

I will leave all gates as found.

I will build fires in designated or safe places only and will be certain they are completely extinguished before leaving the area.

I will discard no burning material - matches, cigarettes, etc.

I will fill all excavation holes which may be dangerous to livestock.

I will not contaminate wells, creeks, or other water supply.

I will cause no willful damage to collecting material and will take home only what I can reasonably use.

I will support the rockhound project H.E.L.P. (Help Eliminate Litter Please) and will leave all collecting areas devoid of litter, regardless of how found.

I will cooperate with field trip leaders and those in designated authority in all collecting areas.

I will report to my club or federation officers, Bureau of Land Management, or other proper authorities, any deposit of petrified wood or other material on public lands which should be protected for the enjoyment of future generations for public educational and scientific purposes.

I will appreciate and protect our heritage of natural resources.

I will observe the "Golden Rule," will use "Good Outdoor Manners" and will at all times conduct myself in a manner which will add to the stature and "Public Image" of rockhounds everywhere.

MINERAL LOCATOR INDEX

Other Titles in the Gem Trail Series

- GEM TRAILS OF ARIZONA, *Mitchell*
  184 pgs., $9.95

- GEM TRAILS OF COLORADO, *Mitchell*
  144 pgs., $9.95

- GEM TRAILS OF NEVADA, *Mitchell*
  119 pgs., $6.95

- GEM TRAILS OF NEW MEXICO, *Mitchell*
  160 pgs., $9.95

- GEM TRAILS OF NORTHERN CALIFORNIA, *Mitchell*
  160 pgs., $9.95

- GEM TRAILS OF PENNSYLVANIA AND NEW JERSEY,
  Stepanski & Snow
  160 pgs., $10.95

- GEM TRAILS OF SOUTHERN CALIFORNIA, *Mitchell*
  184 pgs., $8.95

- GEM TRAILS OF TEXAS, *Mitchell*
  104 pgs., $6.95

- GEM TRAILS OF UTAH, *Mitchell*
  168 pgs., $9.95

- MIDWEST GEM, FOSSIL AND MINERAL TRAILS:
  Great Lakes States, *Zeitner*
  96 pgs., $7.95

- MIDWEST GEM, FOSSIL AND MINERAL TRAILS:
  Prairie States, *Zeitner*
  128 pgs., $9.95

NOTES

NOTES

NOTES